Oxford
Better
French

OXFORD
UNIVERSITY PRESS

Great Clarendon Street, Oxford, OX2 6DP, United Kingdom

Oxford University Press is a department of the University of Oxford.
It furthers the University's objective of excellence in research, scholarship,
and education by publishing worldwide. Oxford is a registered trade mark of
Oxford University Press in the UK and in certain other countries

British Library Cataloguing in Publication Data

Data available

ISBN: 978-0-19-274634-4

1 3 5 7 9 10 8 6 4 2

Printed in China

Paper used in the production of this book is a natural,
recyclable product made from wood grown in sustainable forests.
The manufacturing process conforms to the environmental
regulations of the country of origin.

With thanks to Laurence Larroche, Anna Stevenson,
and Florence Bonneau for support

Introduction

How to use this book

Better French has been written for children aged 11–14. It aims to build vocabulary and reinforce language skills that children learn in school.

The book is split into 3 sections:

Vocabulary: has words in themes often discussed in the classroom, progressing from beginner level to more advanced.

Grammar: includes connecting words, question words, adjectives, pronouns, and regular and irregular verbs.

Conversation: gives questions and answers and shows how to say yes or no to a question.

Each section has engaging word activities at the end to consolidate the information:

- **Spelling help**: reinforces common spelling rules.
- **Word fun**: includes anagrams and word play.
- **Now practise**: focuses on regular usage and topics for conversation.

This structured approach gives practical support to build language skills for school, for holidays and travel, and for life.

Contents

Vocabulaire Vocabulary

Les nombres Numbers 8

Les couleurs Colours 9

Le temps et l'heure Time 10–13

Les animaux sauvages Wild animals 14

Les animaux de compagnie et de la ferme
Pets and farm animals 15

La nourriture et les boissons Food and drink 16–18

Les fruits et les légumes Fruit and vegetables 19

Les repas Meals 20

Mes habitudes quotidiennes My daily routine 21

Les vêtements et les accessoires
Clothes and accessories 22–23

Les parties du corps Parts of the body 24–25

La famille et les amis Family and friends 26–27

Décrire les choses Describing things 28–29

Décrire les gens Describing people 30–31

Décrire ma personnalité Describing my personality 32–33

Ma maison My house 34–35

Dans la salle de classe In the classroom 36–37

Les matières scolaires School subjects 38–39

Le sport Sport 40–41

Le temps libre Free time 42–43

Les métiers Jobs 44–45

Au bord de la mer At the seaside 46–47

Les vacances et les voyages Holidays and travel 48–49

Les moyens de transport Means of transport 50–51

En ville In town 52–53

Les pays, les continents, les langues
Countries, continents, languages 54–55

- Spelling help 56
- Word fun 57
- Now practise 58

Grammaire Grammar

Les questions Questions 60
Les mots de liaison Connecting words 61
Comparer les gens et les choses
Comparing people and things 62
La quantité et l'intensité Quantity and intensity 63
Le temps Time 64–65
La position Position 66–67
Les pronoms personnels Personal pronouns 68–69
Les possessifs Possessives 70–71
Les adjectifs: masculin et féminin
Adjectives: masculine and feminine 72
Expressions avec 'avoir' Expressions with 'avoir' 73
Verbes réguliers Regular verbs 74–75
Verbes irréguliers Irregular verbs 76–82

- Word fun 83
- Now practise 84

Conversation Conversation

Comment ça va? How are you? 86
Rencontrer quelqu'un Meeting someone 87
La famille Family 88
Les goûts et les opinions Likes, dislikes, and opinions 89
L'heure Time 90
Les loisirs Free time 91
La nourriture Food 92
Les vacances Holidays 93

- Now practise 94–95

Vocabulaire
Vocabulary

Les nombres
Numbers

1	un	16	seize	71	soixante-et-onze
2	deux	17	dix-sept	72	soixante-douze
3	trois	18	dix-huit	73	soixante-treize
4	quatre	19	dix-neuf	80	quatre-vingts
5	cinq	20	vingt	81	quatre-vingt-un
6	six	21	vingt et un	82	quatre-vingt-deux
7	sept	22	vingt-deux	83	quatre-vingt-trois
8	huit	23	vingt-trois	90	quatre-vingt-dix
9	neuf	24	vingt-quatre	91	quatre-vingt-onze
10	dix	25	vingt-cinq	92	quatre-vingt-douze
11	onze	30	trente	93	quatre-vingt-treize
12	douze	40	quarante	100	cent
13	treize	50	cinquante	1000	mille
14	quatorze	60	soixante		
15	quinze	70	soixante-dix		

premier, première first	**cinquième** fifth	**neuvième** ninth
deuxième, second(e) second	**sixième** sixth	**dixième** tenth
troisième third	**septième** seventh	
quatrième fourth	**huitième** eighth	

Les couleurs
Colours

bleu, bleue blue	J'ai un scooter **bleu**/une voiture **bleue**. I have a blue scooter/a blue car.
blanc, blanche white	J'ai un foulard **blanc**/des chaussures **blanches**. I have a white scarf/white shoes.
rouge red	Tu es tout **rouge**, tu as trop chaud? You're all red in the face – are you too hot?
jaune yellow	Les fleurs de cette plante sont **jaunes**. The flowers on this plant are yellow.
vert, verte green	C'est un mur **vert**/une maison **verte**. This is a green wall/a green house.
orange orange	Idriss porte un tee-shirt **orange**. Idriss is wearing an orange T-shirt.
gris, grise grey	Je vois un cahier **gris**/une couverture **grise**. I see a grey exercise book/a grey cover.
marron brown	Mon frère a les yeux **marron**. My brother has brown eyes.
rose pink	Il y a des fleurs **roses** dans le jardin. There are pink flowers in the garden.
violet, violette purple	Elle porte un pantalon **violet**/des lunettes **violettes**. She wears purple trousers/purple glasses.
foncé dark	À l'école, je porte un pull bleu **foncé**. In school, I wear a dark blue jumper.
clair light	Le directeur porte une cravate bleu **clair**. The headmaster wears a light blue tie.

Top tip: Some words are different in the masculine and the feminine (**bleu/bleue**) and in the plural (**jaunes**); some remain the same (**marron**).

Le temps et l'heure
Time

heure hour/time	Le film dure deux **heures**./Quelle **heure** est-il? The film is two hours long./What time is it?
minute minute	Je reviens dans deux **minutes**. I'll be back in a couple of minutes.
seconde second	Attends une **seconde**! Wait a second!
jour day	Je fais de la musique tous les **jours**. I play music every day.
journée day	Ne m'appelle pas pendant la **journée**. Don't call me during the day.
semaine week	Je n'ai pas vu Samira cette **semaine**. I haven't seen Samira this week.
mois month	Son bébé a trois **mois**. Her baby is three months old.
an year	Il a treize **ans**. He's thirteen (years old).
année year	En France, l'**année** scolaire va de septembre à juin. In France, the school year runs from September to June.
siècle century	Nous sommes au vingt-et-unième **siècle**. We're in the twenty-first century.
date date	On doit écrire la **date** en haut de la page. We have to write the date at the top of the page.

Le temps et l'heure
Time

moment moment/time	Il y a du brouillard en ce **moment**/On a passé un bon **moment** ensemble. It's foggy at the moment/We had a good time together.
dernier, dernière last	On a joué au foot la semaine **dernière**. We played football last week.
hier yesterday	Il a plu **hier**. It rained yesterday.
aujourd'hui today	C'est lundi **aujourd'hui**. It's Monday today.
demain tomorrow	Je dois dire au revoir à mon ami **demain**. I have to say goodbye to my friend tomorrow.
prochain, prochaine next	L'année **prochaine**, nous irons en vacances en Espagne. Next year we'll go on holiday to Spain.

Les saisons
Seasons

printemps spring	**automne** autumn
été summer	**hiver** winter
Ici, il commence à neiger vers le début de l'**hiver**. It begins to snow here quite early in the winter.	Les arbres fleurissent au **printemps**. The trees flower in the spring.

Le temps et l'heure
Time

Les mois
Months

janvier January	**avril** April	**juillet** July	**octobre** October
février February	**mai** May	**août** August	**novembre** November
mars March	**juin** June	**septembre** September	**décembre** December
En **mars**, au mois de **mars**		In March	

Les jours de la semaine
Days of the week

lundi Monday	**jeudi** Thursday	**dimanche** Sunday	**cette semaine** this week
mardi Tuesday	**vendredi** Friday	**après-demain** the day after tomorrow	**la semaine prochaine** next week
mercredi Wednesday	**samedi** Saturday	**avant-hier** the day before yesterday	**la semaine dernière** last week

On se retrouve **samedi?** Shall we meet up on Saturday?	J'ai cours de piano le **mardi**. I have a piano lesson on Tuesdays.
Je vais à la piscine tous les **mercredis**. I go to the swimming pool every Wednesday.	Mes parents sont rentrés **avant-hier**. My parents came home the day before yesterday.

Le temps et l'heure
Time

La journée
Times of day

aube dawn	Ils sont partis à l'**aube**. They left at dawn.
matin morning	Tu t'es levé à quelle heure ce **matin**? What time did you get up this morning?
midi midday	Je t'appellerai à **midi**. I'll call you at midday.
après-midi afternoon	On a passé tout l'**après-midi** à raconter des histoires drôles. We spent the whole afternoon telling funny stories.
soir evening	Il fait froid le **soir**. It's cold in the evening.
ce soir tonight	On sort **ce soir**? Shall we go out tonight?
soirée evening	Je passerai chez toi dans la **soirée**. I'll pop round to yours in the evening.
nuit night	Il a plu toute la **nuit**. It rained all night.
minuit midnight	Il est déjà **minuit**, il faut rentrer. It's already midnight – we have to go home.

Top tip: In French, the names of days and months do not start with a capital letter.

Les animaux sauvages
Wild animals

éléphant elephant	L'**éléphant** est le plus gros animal terrestre. The elephant is the largest land animal.
crocodile crocodile	Le **crocodile** est un reptile. Crocodiles are reptiles.
lion lion	Le **lion** a attaqué une gazelle. The lion attacked a gazelle.
tigre tiger	Le **tigre** blanc est une espèce en danger. The white tiger is an endangered species.
girafe giraffe	Le cou de la **girafe** mesure environ trois mètres. The neck of a giraffe is around three metres long.
serpent snake	Attention, il y a des **serpents** dans l'herbe. Be careful, there are snakes in the grass.
singe monkey	Les **singes** du zoo sont très bruyants. The monkeys in the zoo are very noisy.
zèbre zebra	Le **zèbre** appartient à la même famille que le cheval. The zebra belongs to the same family as the horse.
rhinocéros rhino(ceros)	En Afrique, il y a des **rhinocéros** blancs et des **rhinocéros** noirs. In Africa there are white rhinos and black rhinos.
hippopotame hippo(potamus)	Les **hippopotames** prennent des bains de boue. Hippos have mud baths.
kangourou kangaroo	Les **kangourous** portent leurs bébés dans une poche. Kangaroos carry their babies in a pouch.
pingouin penguin	Il reste quelques **pingouins** en Bretagne. There are a few penguins left in Brittany.

Les animaux de compagnie et de la ferme
Pets and farm animals

chien dog	Mon **chien** est un labrador. My dog is a labrador.
chat cat	J'ai un **chat**, il s'appelle Lucifer. I have a cat – his name is Lucifer.
poisson (rouge) (gold)fish	Sur la table, il y a un bocal avec des **poissons rouges**. On the table, there's a bowl with goldfish in it.
tortue tortoise	Ma **tortue** aime manger des fleurs. My tortoise likes to eat flowers.
cochon d'Inde guinea pig	Nous avons un **cochon d'Inde** femelle. We have a female guinea pig.
oiseau bird	L'**oiseau** chante toute la journée dans sa cage. The bird sings all day long in its cage.
lapin rabbit	On a un gros **lapin** blanc dans le jardin. We have a big white rabbit in the garden.
cheval horse	Est-ce que tu fais du **cheval**? Do you go horse-riding?
vache cow	Les **vaches** et leurs veaux sont dans le champ. The cows and their calves are in the field.
mouton sheep	On a vu passer un troupeau de **moutons**. We saw a flock of sheep go past.
poule hen	Nos **poules** mangent surtout du maïs. Our hens eat mostly maize.
canard duck	Les **canards** sont dans la mare. The ducks are in the pond.

La nourriture et les boissons
Food and drink

pain bread	Les Français mangent beaucoup de **pain** aux repas. The French eat a lot of bread with their meals.
fromage cheese	**Fromage** ou dessert? Cheese or pudding?
viande meat	Je ne mange pas de **viande**, je suis végétarien. I don't eat meat, I'm vegetarian.
jambon ham	Je voudrais un sandwich au **jambon**, s'il vous plaît. I would like a ham sandwich, please.
poulet chicken	J'ai commandé du **poulet**-frites. I ordered chicken with chips.
saucisse sausage	Les merguez sont des **saucisses** de bœuf et de mouton. Merguez are sausages made with beef and mutton.
rôti roast	Ce **rôti** de bœuf est délicieux. This roast beef is delicious.
pizza pizza	Une part de **pizza** aux champignons, s'il vous plaît. A slice of mushroom pizza, please.
riz rice	J'adore le **riz** cantonais. I love egg fried rice.
pâtes pasta	Ces **pâtes** sont très bonnes. This pasta is very good.
spaghettis spaghetti	Ces **spaghettis** sont froids. This spaghetti is cold.
frites chips	J'aime bien mettre du ketchup sur mes **frites**. I like to put ketchup on my chips.

La nourriture et les boissons
Food and drink

soupe soup	Il y a de la **soupe** de légumes comme entrée. There's vegetable soup as a starter.
œuf egg	On a mangé des **œufs** sur le plat hier soir. We ate fried eggs last night.
gâteau cake	Son **gâteau** d'anniversaire est magnifique. Her birthday cake is beautiful.
yaourt yogurt	Tu veux un **yaourt** nature ou à la fraise? Do you want a natural yogurt or a strawberry one?
glace ice cream	J'ai de la **glace** à la vanille, à la fraise et au chocolat. I have vanilla, strawberry, and chocolate ice cream.
crêpe pancake	On a acheté des **crêpes** au Nutella® au marché. We bought Nutella® pancakes at the market.
biscuit biscuit	Nico a mangé deux paquets de **biscuits**! Nico ate two packets of biscuits!
chocolat chocolate	Le chocolat au lait est plus sucré que le **chocolat** noir. Milk chocolate is sweeter than dark chocolate.
bonbons sweets	Mes parents ne me laissent pas manger trop de **bonbons**. My parents don't let me eat too many sweets.
chips crisps	On a emporté des **chips** pour le pique-nique. We took crisps for the picnic.
sel salt	Trop de **sel** est mauvais pour la santé. Too much salt is bad for you.
poivre pepper	Il y a trop de **poivre** sur ce steak. There's too much pepper on this steak.

Vocabulaire

sucre sugar	Elle ne prend jamais de **sucre** dans son café. She never has sugar in her coffee.
beurre butter	Il n'y a pas assez de **beurre** dans ce sandwich. There isn't enough butter in this sandwich.
confiture jam	Des tartines grillées avec de la **confiture** de fraise. Toast with strawberry jam.
céréales cereal	Il y a des **céréales** au petit déjeuner. There is cereal at breakfast.
lait milk	Je bois un verre de **lait** chaud avant de me coucher. I drink a glass of warm milk before going to bed.
chocolat chaud hot chocolate	Il nous a proposé un **chocolat chaud** avec des guimauves. He offered us a hot chocolate with marshmallows.
jus de fruit fruit juice	Qu'est-ce que vous avez comme **jus de fruit**? What kinds of fruit juice do you have?
thé tea	Les Anglais boivent plus de **thé** que les Français. The English drink more tea than the French.
café coffee	Un **café** noir ou au lait? A black coffee or one with milk?
eau water	Nous buvons toujours de l'**eau** à table. We always drink water at mealtimes.
coca Coke®	Un **coca**, s'il vous plaît. A Coke®, please.
limonade lemonade	Deux **limonades** et un jus d'orange, s'il vous plaît. Two lemonades and one orange juice, please.

Les fruits et les légumes
Fruit and vegetables

pomme apple	La **pomme** est mon fruit préféré. Apples are my favourite fruit.
orange orange	J'aime les **oranges** quand elles sont juteuses. I like oranges when they're juicy.
banane banana	Elle met des **bananes** dans la salade de fruits. She puts bananas in fruit salads.
poire pear	Un kilo de **poires**, s'il vous plaît. A kilo of pears, please.
pêche peach	Je vais faire une tarte aux **pêches** pour le dessert. I'm going to make a peach tart for dessert.
fraise strawberry	Ces **fraises** ne sont pas mûres. These strawberries are not ripe.
pomme de terre potato	Il faut couper les **pommes de terre** en tranches fines. You have to cut the potatoes into thin slices.
carotte carrot	On mange souvent des **carottes** râpées à la cantine. We often have grated carrots in our school dinners.
oignon onion	Je déteste l'**oignon** cru. I hate raw onion.
tomate tomato	Je prendrai la salade de **tomates**. I'll have the tomato salad.
laitue, salade lettuce	Mon père cultive des **laitues** dans son jardin. My father grows lettuces in his garden.
haricots verts green beans	Les **haricots verts** vont bien avec le rôti. Green beans go well with a roast.

Les repas
Meals

petit déjeuner breakfast	Ils servent le **petit déjeuner** entre 7 heures et 9 heures. They serve breakfast between 7 and 9.
déjeuner lunch	Tu manges toujours un sandwich au **déjeuner**? Do you always have a sandwich for lunch?
goûter afternoon snack	Loïc a fait un gâteau pour le **goûter**. Loïc baked a cake to have as an afternoon snack.
dîner dinner	Le **dîner** était excellent. Dinner was excellent.
plat dish	C'est un **plat** très facile à préparer. It's a very easy dish to make.
entrée first course, starter	Qu'est-ce que vous prendrez comme **entrée**? What will you have as a starter?
plat principal main course	Pour le **plat principal**, il y a du poisson ou du rôti. For the main course, there's fish or a roast.
dessert dessert	Je ne prendrai pas de **dessert**. I won't have a dessert.
assiette plate	Tu as oublié les **assiettes** à soupe. You forgot the soup plates.
couteau knife	Le **couteau** se met à droite de l'assiette. The knife goes to the right of the plate.
fourchette fork	Tu préfères une **fourchette** ou des baguettes? Would you prefer a fork or chopsticks?
cuillère, cuiller spoon	Ces **cuillères** à café sont en argent. These coffee spoons are made of silver.

Mes habitudes quotidiennes
My daily routine

se réveiller to wake up	Je **me réveille**. I wake up.
se lever to get up	Je **me lève**. I get up.
s'habiller to get dressed	Je **m'habille**. I get dressed.
prendre son petit déjeuner to have breakfast	Je **prends mon petit déjeuner**. I have breakfast.
se brosser les dents to brush one's teeth	Je **me brosse les dents**. I brush my teeth.
se coiffer to brush one's hair	Je **me coiffe**. I brush my hair.
aller à l'école à pied/en bus to walk/to take the bus to school	Je **vais à l'école à pied/en bus**. I walk/take the bus to school.
faire ses devoirs to do one's homework	Je **fais mes devoirs**. I do my homework.
se laver to wash oneself	Je **me lave**. I wash myself.
se doucher to have a shower	Je **me douche**. I have a shower.
se coucher to go to bed	Je **me couche**. I go to bed.
s'endormir to go to sleep	Je **m'endors**. I go to sleep.

Top tip: Some words are spelled differently but sound the same, e.g. **cuillère** and **cuiller** both end with the sound /air/.

Les vêtements et les accessoires
Clothes and accessories

pantalon trousers	Ce **pantalon** est trop étroit. Those trousers are too tight.
jean jeans	Mon **jean** est troué. My jeans have got a hole in them.
short shorts	Il fait très chaud, je mets un **short**. It's very hot – I'm putting shorts on.
jupe skirt	La **jupe** de notre uniforme est grise. Our uniform skirt is grey.
robe dress	Cette **robe** te va super bien. That dress really suits you.
pull jumper, sweater	Mets un **pull**, il fait froid dehors. Put a jumper on – it's cold outside.
sweat(-shirt) sweatshirt	Tu aimes mon nouveau **sweat**? Do you like my new sweatshirt?
tee-shirt T-shirt	Malik s'est acheté un **tee-shirt** noir. Malik bought himself a black T-shirt.
chemise shirt	Mon père porte une **chemise** pour aller au travail. My father wears a shirt for work.
blouson jacket	J'aimerais avoir un **blouson** en cuir. I would like a leather jacket.
veste jacket	C'est la mode des **vestes** en fausse fourrure. Faux fur jackets are fashionable.
gilet cardigan	Je peux te prêter un **gilet** si tu as froid. I can lend you a cardigan if you're cold.

Les vêtements et les accessoires
Clothes and accessories

pyjama pyjamas	Mettez-vous en **pyjama**, les enfants. Put your pyjamas on, children.
cravate tie	On doit porter une **cravate** au lycée. We have to wear a tie at school.
écharpe scarf	J'ai laissé mon **écharpe** dans le bus. I left my scarf on the bus.
bonnet (woolly) hat	Il neige, n'oublie pas ton **bonnet**. It's snowing – don't forget your hat.
gants gloves	Ces **gants** en laine sont très chauds. These woollen gloves are very warm.
casquette (baseball) cap	Il est rigolo avec sa **casquette** fluo. He looks funny with his fluorescent baseball cap.
ceinture belt	Mon jean est trop grand, il me faut une **ceinture**. My jeans are too big – I need a belt.
lunettes de soleil sunglasses	À qui sont ces **lunettes de soleil**? Whose sunglasses are these?
chaussettes socks	Alice ne porte jamais de **chaussettes**, même en hiver. Alice never wears socks, not even in winter.
chaussures shoes	Il y a un magasin de **chaussures** dans le centre commercial. There is a shoe shop in the shopping centre.
baskets trainers	Quentin a toujours des **baskets** super chères. Quentin always has really expensive trainers.
bottes boots	Vous avez ces **bottes** en 38? Do you have these boots in a size 5?

Top tip: Words like *trousers*, *jeans* or *pyjamas* are plural in English but singular in French: **le pantalon, le jean, le pyjama**.

Les parties du corps
Parts of the body

tête head	J'ai mal à la **tête**. I have a headache.
cou neck	Elle a un très long **cou**. She has a very long neck.
épaule shoulder	On a fait des exercices pour décontracter les **épaules**. We did some exercises to relax our shoulders.
dos back	Couchez-vous sur le **dos**. Lie down on your back.
poitrine chest	Il a la **poitrine** assez large. He has quite a broad chest.
ventre stomach	Arrête de manger si tu as mal au **ventre**. Stop eating if you have stomach ache.
bras arm	Clara m'a attrapé par le **bras**. Clara grabbed me by the arm.
jambe leg	Il a été blessé à la **jambe** gauche. He hurt his left leg.
pied foot	Guillaume a de grands **pieds**, il fait du 46. Guillaume has big feet, he takes a size 11.
main hand	Ils m'ont serré la **main** quand je suis arrivé. They shook my hand when I arrived.
doigt finger	Cette bague est trop large pour mon **doigt**. This ring is too big for my finger.
orteil toe	Aïe, je me suis cogné l'**orteil**! Ouch, I stubbed my toe!

genou knee	Je me suis fait mal au **genou** en tombant. I hurt my knee when I fell.
fesses bottom	Il m'a donné un coup de pied aux **fesses**! He kicked me on the bottom!
coude elbow	Ne mets pas tes **coudes** sur la table quand tu manges. Don't put your elbows on the table when you eat.
œil (les yeux) eye	Mia a de beaux **yeux** gris. Mia has beautiful grey eyes.
nez nose	J'ai le **nez** bouché. My nose is blocked.
bouche mouth	Ne parle pas la **bouche** pleine! Don't speak with your mouth full!
oreille ear	Il faut mettre un bonnet pour se protéger les **oreilles**. You have to wear a hat to protect your ears.
cheveux hair	Je me lave les **cheveux** deux fois par semaine. I wash my hair twice a week.
menton chin	Il se frotte le **menton** quand il réfléchit. He rubs his chin when he's thinking.
dent tooth	Ahmed a mal aux **dents**. Ahmed has toothache.
langue tongue	Je me suis brûlé la **langue** en mangeant de la soupe. I burnt my tongue eating soup.
visage face	Ce **visage** me dit quelque chose. This face looks familiar.

La famille et les amis
Family and friends

père father, dad	Mon **père** a quarante-trois ans. My father is forty-three.
mère mother, mum	Ma **mère** travaille dans un bureau. My mother works in an office.
parents parents	Je m'entends assez bien avec mes **parents**. I get on quite well with my parents.
frère brother	Mon **frère** a deux ans de plus que moi. My brother is two years older than me.
sœur sister	J'ai une grande **sœur** et une petite **sœur**. I have an older sister and a younger sister.
demi-frère half-brother	J'ai un **demi-frère** qui habite avec nous. I have a half-brother who lives with us.
demi-sœur half-sister	Ma **demi-sœur** s'appelle Anaïs. My half-sister's name is Anaïs.
grand-père grandfather	Mon **grand-père** était architecte. My grandfather was an architect.
grand-mère grandmother	Ma **grand-mère** a soixante-cinq ans. My grandmother is sixty-five.
grands-parents grandparents	Je suis allé à la mer avec mes **grands-parents**. I went to the seaside with my grandparents.
fils son	Je joue au foot avec le **fils** des voisins. I play football with the neighbours' son.
fille daughter	C'est la **fille** de ma prof de maths. She's my maths teacher's daughter.

La famille et les amis
Family and friends

fils unique, fille unique only child	Je suis **fils unique/fille unique**. I'm an only child.
cousin, cousine cousin	J'ai douze **cousins**. I have twelve cousins.
oncle uncle	On va chez mon **oncle** ce week-end. We're going to my uncle's this weekend.
tante aunt	Ma **tante** n'a que cinq ans de plus que moi. My aunt is only five years older than me.
beau-père stepfather, stepdad	Je m'entends bien avec mon **beau-père**. I get on well with my stepfather.
belle-mère stepmother, stepmum	Ma **belle-mère** a deux enfants. My stepmother has two children.
ami, amie friend	Je me suis fait des **amis** français pendant les vacances. I made some French friends during the holidays.
copain, copine friend, mate	Je sors souvent avec mes **copines**. I often go out with my friends.
bande group	J'ai une super **bande** de copains. I have a great group of friends.
proche close	J'ai deux amis **proches**. I have two close friends.
petit copain boyfriend	Leïla a un **petit copain** irlandais. Leïla has an Irish boyfriend.
petite copine girlfriend	Tu as une **petite copine**? Do you have a girlfriend?

grand, grande big, large	Bordeaux est une **grande** ville. Bordeaux is a big city.
petit, petite small, little	Leur maison est assez **petite**. Their house is quite small.
long, longue long	Tu n'as pas trouvé le film un peu **long**? Did you not think the film was a bit long?
court, courte short	Cette jupe est trop **courte**. This skirt is too short.
large wide	Le jardin est très **large**. The garden is very wide.
étroit, étroite narrow	Les rues de la vieille ville sont **étroites**. The streets in the old town are narrow.
vieux, vieille old	C'est le plus **vieux** pont du pays. It's the oldest bridge in the country.
neuf, neuve new	Antoine a un vélo tout **neuf**. Antoine has a brand new bicycle.
ancien, ancienne old	Ils ont des meubles **anciens** dans leur salon. They have old furniture in their living room.
moderne modern	J'aime les bâtiments **modernes**. I like modern buildings.
beau, belle beautiful	Que c'est **beau** ici! It's so beautiful here!
joli, jolie pretty	On a visité un **joli** petit village. We visited a pretty little village.

Décrire les choses
Describing things

moche ugly	Ce tableau est vraiment **moche**. This painting is really ugly.
bon, bonne good	J'ai trouvé le repas super **bon**. I thought the meal was very good.
mauvais, mauvaise bad	Son dernier film n'est pas **mauvais**. Her latest film isn't bad.
bien good	Il est **bien**, ce jeu vidéo? Is this video game good?
super great	Tu as vu notre spectacle? Il était **super**, non? Did you see our show? It was great, wasn't it?
nul, nulle rubbish	Cette BD est archi-**nulle**. This comic is absolutely rubbish.
délicieux, **délicieuse** delicious	Merci pour ce **délicieux** repas. Thank you for this delicious meal.
confortable comfortable	Les lits de l'hôtel ne sont pas **confortables**. The hotel beds are not comfortable.
fatigant, fatigante tiring	J'espère que le voyage n'a pas été trop **fatigant**. I hope the journey wasn't too tiring.
facile easy	Trop **facile**, le contrôle de maths! The maths test was really easy!
difficile difficult	Vous trouvez que le français est une langue **difficile**? Do you think French is a difficult language?
intéressant, **intéressante** interesting	C'est une histoire vraiment **intéressante**. It's a really interesting story.

Décrire les gens
Describing people

grand, grande tall	Clémentine est **grande** pour son âge. Clémentine is tall for her age.
petit, petite small, short	C'est le plus **petit** de la classe. He's the shortest in the class.
gros, grosse fat	Mon voisin est **gros** et chauve. My neighbour is fat and bald.
mince slim	Pour être **mince**, il faut manger équilibré. To be slim, you have to eat a balanced diet.
maigre skinny	Elle est un peu **maigre**. She's a bit skinny.
brun, brune dark-haired	C'est un garçon **brun** aux yeux bleus. He's a dark-haired boy with blue eyes.
blond, blonde fair	Marie est **blonde**. Marie has fair hair.
roux, rousse red	Ron Weasley est **roux**. Ron Weasley has red hair.
gentil, gentille kind	J'essaie d'être **gentil** avec tout le monde. I try to be kind to everyone.
méchant, méchante mean, nasty	Ne sois pas si **méchante** avec elle! Don't be so mean to her!
désagréable unpleasant	Il peut être **désagréable** quand il est fâché. He can be unpleasant when he's cross.
sympa nice	Il est **sympa**, ton copain. Your friend's nice.

Décrire les gens
Describing people

timide shy	Vas-y, ne sois pas **timide**. Go on, don't be shy.
rigolo, rigolote funny	Qu'est-ce qu'il est **rigolo**, celui-là! He's so funny, that one!
généreux, généreuse generous	Elle est **généreuse**, elle prête facilement ses affaires. She's generous – she's happy to lend her things.
égoïste selfish	Il est hyper **égoïste**. He's really selfish.
intelligent, intelligente clever	C'est une fille très **intelligente**. She's a very intelligent girl.
sportif, sportive sporty	Beaucoup d'élèves de ma classe sont très **sportifs**. Many students in my class are very sporty.
travailleur, travailleuse hard-working	Elle a de bonnes notes parce qu'elle est **travailleuse**. She gets good marks because she's hard-working.
paresseux, paresseuse lazy	La prof m'a dit que j'étais **paresseux**. The teacher told me I was lazy.
têtu, têtue stubborn	Ce que tu peux être **têtu**! You can be so stubborn!
curieux, curieuse curious	Basile est très **curieux**, il veut connaître mon secret. Basile is very curious – he wants to know my secret.
bavard, bavarde talkative	Ils sont sympas mais un peu trop **bavards** en classe. They're nice but a bit too talkative in class.

Top tip: In French, the word **cheveux** (*hair*) is not normally used when describing hair colour – you often simply say **roux/rousse** or **brun/brune**.

Décrire ma personnalité
Describing my personality

qualité quality	Mon prof dit que j'ai beaucoup de **qualités**. My teacher says I have many good qualities.
défaut fault	J'ai un **défaut**: je suis très bavard. I have one fault: I'm very talkative.
goûts tastes	Max n'a pas les mêmes **goûts** musicaux que moi. Max doesn't have the same musical tastes as me.
caractère character	Tu trouves que j'ai un fort **caractère**? Do you think I have a strong character?
avoir bon/mauvais caractère to be good-natured/ bad-tempered	Mes copains disent que j'ai **bon/ mauvais caractère**. My friends say that I'm rather good-natured/ bad-tempered.
calme calm	Je suis quelqu'un de **calme**, je m'énerve rarement. I'm a calm person – I rarely lose my temper.
patient, patiente patient	J'aimerais être plus **patient**, mais c'est difficile. I'd like to be more patient, but it's difficult.
impatient, impatiente impatient	Je suis très **impatiente**, je déteste attendre. I'm very impatient – I hate waiting.
nerveux, nerveuse nervous	Je suis trop **nerveux**, j'ai du mal à me calmer. I'm too nervous – I find it hard to calm down.
positif, positive positive	J'essaie toujours d'être **positif**. I always try to be positive.
actif, active active	Je suis très **active**, je fais plein de choses le week-end. I'm very active – I do a lot of things at the weekend.

Décrire ma personnalité
Describing my personality

tolérant, tolérante tolerant	J'essaie d'être **tolérant** et d'accepter les différences. I try to be tolerant and to accept differences.
ouvert, ouverte open-minded	J'espère que les gens me trouvent **ouvert**. I hope people think I'm open-minded.
courageux, courageuse brave	Je pense être plus **courageuse** que quand j'étais petite. I think I'm braver now than when I was little.
sérieux, sérieuse serious	Mon frère dit que je suis trop **sérieux**. My brother says I'm too serious.
avoir de l'humour to have a sense of humour	Il est important d'**avoir de l'humour**. It's important to have a sense of humour.
sociable outgoing	Je suis **sociable**, je me fais facilement des amis. I'm outgoing – I make friends easily.
franc, franche frank	Certains me trouvent trop **franche**. Some people think I'm too frank.
sensible sensitive	Les films tristes me font pleurer, je suis très **sensible**. Sad films make me cry – I'm very sensitive.
peureux, peureuse easily scared	Ma sœur dit que je suis **peureux**. My sister says I'm easily scared.
râleur, râleuse who moans a lot	Oui, je sais, je suis **râleur**. Yes, I know, I moan a lot.
imagination imagination	Mon prof dit que j'ai beaucoup d'**imagination**. My teacher says I have a lot of imagination.
créatif, créative creative	Je suis plus créative que sportive. I'm more creative than sporty.

Ma maison
My house

étage floor	Ma maison a deux **étages**. My house has two floors.
rez-de-chaussée ground floor	Ma chambre est au **rez-de-chaussée**. My bedroom is on the ground floor.
cave cellar	Ils ont aménagé une salle de jeux dans la **cave**. They put a games room in the cellar.
pièce room	C'est un appartement de cinq **pièces**. It's a flat with five rooms.
chambre bedroom	Il y a trois **chambres** au premier étage. There are three bedrooms on the first floor.
cuisine kitchen	La **cuisine** est toute petite. The kitchen is very small.
salon living room	On se retrouve au **salon** pour regarder la télé. We get together in the living room to watch TV.
salle à manger dining room	Il n'y a pas de **salle à manger**, on mange à la cuisine. There is no dining room – we eat in the kitchen.
salle de bains bathroom	Il y a combien de **salles de bains** chez toi? How many bathrooms are there in your house?
jardin garden	En Angleterre, la plupart des maisons ont un **jardin**. In England, most houses have a garden.
garage garage	Nous garons notre voiture dans le **garage**. We park our car in the garage.
escalier stairs	L'**escalier** est étroit. The stairs are narrow.

Ma maison
My house

porte door	Je ferme toujours ma **porte** à clé. I always lock my door.
fenêtre window	Il y a une grande **fenêtre** dans ma chambre. There's a big window in my bedroom.
balcon balcony	C'est un appartement avec un long **balcon**. It's a flat with a long balcony.
table table	On mange toujours à **table** chez moi. At my house we always eat at the table.
chaise chair	La **chaise** est contre le mur. The chair is against the wall.
fauteuil (arm)chair	J'ai un **fauteuil** hyper confortable dans ma chambre. I have a really comfortable armchair in my bedroom.
canapé sofa	C'est un **canapé** quatre places. It's a four-seater sofa.
lampe lamp	Tu as une **lampe** dans ta chambre? Do you have a lamp in your bedroom?
lit bed	Ma sœur et moi on dort dans des **lits** superposés. Ma sister and I sleep in bunk beds.
appartement flat	Tu habites dans une maison ou un **appartement**? Do you live in a house or a flat?
immeuble building	C'est un **immeuble** de vingt étages. It's a twenty-storey building.
lotissement (housing) estate	Ma maison est dans un **lotissement** près de Liverpool. My house is on an estate near Liverpool.

Dans la salle de classe
In the classroom

bureau desk	La prof est assise à son **bureau**. The teacher is sitting at her desk.
tableau blanc whiteboard	Je ne vois pas bien le **tableau blanc**. I can't see the whiteboard very well.
affiche poster	Il y a des **affiches** partout sur les murs. There are posters all over the walls.
ordinateur computer	On utilise souvent les **ordinateurs** en cours. We often use computers in class.
souris mouse	La **souris** ne marche pas. The mouse isn't working.
clavier keyboard	Le **clavier** anglais est différent du **clavier** français. The English keyboard is different from the French keyboard.
écran screen	L'**écran** de l'ordinateur est sale. The computer screen is dirty.
projecteur projector	Le **projecteur** est cassé. The projector is broken.
imprimante printer	Monsieur, je peux utiliser l'**imprimante**? Sir, can I use the printer?
casier locker	J'ai perdu la clé de mon **casier**. I've lost the key to my locker.
sac à dos backpack	Mon **sac à dos** est super lourd aujourd'hui. My backpack is really heavy today.
manuel textbook	Tu me prêtes ton **manuel** de biologie? Can you lend me your biology textbook?

Dans la salle de classe
In the classroom

cahier (exercise) book	Où est mon **cahier** de maths? Where's my maths (exercise) book?
cahier de brouillon notebook	Je vais l'écrire dans mon **cahier de brouillon**. I'm going to write it in my notebook.
carnet (small) notebook	On a un **carnet** pour le vocabulaire. We have a (small) notebook for vocabulary.
papier paper	Il n'y a plus de **papier** dans l'imprimante. There isn't any paper left in the printer.
agenda diary	Tu dois noter tes devoirs dans ton **agenda**. You have to write your homework in your diary.
trousse pencil case	Elle est chouette, ta **trousse**, tu l'as achetée où? Your pencil case is nice – where did you buy it?
crayon pencil	Je dessine toujours au **crayon**. I always draw in pencil.
stylo pen	Quelqu'un a un **stylo** rouge? Does anybody have a red pen?
gomme rubber, eraser	Passe-moi ta **gomme**, s'il te plaît. Pass me your rubber, please.
règle ruler	Il faut une **règle** pour souligner la date. You need a ruler to underline the date.
ciseaux scissors	Michael m'a prêté ses **ciseaux**. Michael lent me his scissors.
calculatrice calculator	Les **calculatrices** sont interdites pendant le contrôle. Calculators are not allowed during the test.

Les matières scolaires
School subjects

français French	Je fais du **français** au collège. I study French at school.
anglais English	Mon prof d'**anglais** est sympa. My English teacher is nice.
maths maths	Tu aimes les **maths**? Do you like maths?
biologie biology	La **biologie** est ma matière préférée. Biology is my favourite subject.
physique physics	Je trouve les cours de **physique** ennuyeux. I think physics lessons are boring.
chimie chemistry	J'ai bien réussi à mon contrôle de **chimie**. I did well in my chemistry test.
sciences science	Comment s'appelle ton prof de **sciences**? What's your science teacher's name?
histoire history	L'**histoire** est une matière passionnante. History is a fascinating subject.
géographie, géo geography	On parle de l'environnement en **géo**. We talk about the environment in geography.
EPS (éducation physique et sportive) PE (physical education)	On a trois heures d'**EPS** par semaine. We have three hours of PE a week.
musique music	J'adore les cours de **musique**. I love music classes.
arts plastiques art	Qu'est-ce que vous faites en **arts plastiques**? What are you doing in art?

Les matières scolaires
School subjects

théâtre drama	On s'amuse bien en cours de **théâtre**. We have fun in our drama classes.
technologie DT (design and technology)	On a **technologie** en salle SL2. We have DT in room SL2.
informatique IT (information technology)	Vous faites de la programmation en **informatique**? Do you do programming in IT?
éducation civique citizenship	Les cours d'**éducation civique** sont intéressants. Citizenship classes are interesting.
programme curriculum	Ce livre n'est pas au **programme**. This book isn't part of the curriculum.
exercice exercise	On doit faire le premier et le deuxième **exercice**. We have to do the first and second exercises.
contrôle test	J'ai un **contrôle** d'anglais mardi prochain. I have an English test next Tuesday.
examen exam	On passe les **examens** de GCSE à 15 ans. You take GCSE exams when you're 15.
exposé presentation	Je dois préparer un **exposé** d'histoire avec Simon. I have to prepare a history presentation with Simon.
dossier project	On fait un **dossier** de sciences cette semaine. We're doing a science project this week.
devoirs homework	Chouette, je n'ai pas de **devoirs**! Great, I don't have any homework to do!
note mark	Tu as eu une bonne **note** en maths? Did you get a good mark in maths?

foot(ball) football	L'équipe de **foot** du collège n'est pas mauvaise. The school football team isn't bad.
rugby rugby	Tu aimerais jouer au **rugby**? Would you like to play rugby?
hand(ball) handball	Les Français jouent beaucoup au **hand**. The French play handball a lot.
volley(ball) volleyball	On fait du **volley** en ce moment en EPS. We're doing volleyball at the moment in PE.
basket(ball) basketball	Mohamed est super grand et il joue au **basket**. Mohamed is very tall and he plays basketball.
tennis tennis	J'aime regarder les championnats de **tennis** à la télé. I like watching tennis championships on TV.
gymnastique gymnastics	Lise est douée en **gymnastique**. Lise is good at gymnastics.
danse classique ballet	Je fais de la **danse classique** depuis cinq ans. I've been doing ballet for five years.
danse moderne modern dance	La **danse moderne** ne m'attire pas. Modern dance doesn't appeal to me.
judo judo	Le **judo** est un sport très pratiqué en France. Judo is a very popular sport in France.
natation swimming	J'ai pris des cours de **natation** pendant des années. I took swimming classes for years.
équitation horse-riding	Il y a un club d'**équitation** près de chez moi. There's a horse-riding club near my house.

Le sport
Sport

cyclisme cycling	Le **cyclisme** a de plus en plus de succès en Angleterre. Cycling is becoming more and more popular in England.
marche walking	La **marche** est un bon exercice. Walking is good exercise.
course (à pied) running	Je fais de la **course (à pied)** trois fois par semaine. I go running three times a week.
faire du ski to ski	On **fait du ski** dans les Alpes tous les hivers. We ski in the Alps every winter.
faire du surf to surf	J'ai appris à **faire du surf** l'été dernier. I learned to surf last summer.
patinage skating	J'adore regarder le **patinage** artistique à la télé. I love watching figure skating on TV.
match match	C'est le dernier **match** de la saison. It's the last match in the season.
tournoi tournament	Notre équipe ne participera pas au **tournoi**. Our team won't take part in the tournament.
championnat championship	Le **championnat** du monde d'athlétisme commence demain. The athletics world championships begin tomorrow.
joueur, joueuse player	Il y a deux **joueuses** blessées. There are two injured players.
entraînement training	J'ai **entraînement** de foot deux fois par semaine. I have football training twice a week.
échauffement warm-up	On commence toujours par un **échauffement**. We always start with a warm-up.

Le temps libre
Free time

Vocabulaire

passe-temps hobby, pastime	Le dessin est mon **passe-temps** préféré. Drawing is my favourite pastime.
loisirs leisure	Le club propose plusieurs activités de **loisirs**. The club offers several leisure activities.
musique music	J'écoute tout le temps de la **musique**. I listen to music all the time.
cinéma cinema	On va au **cinéma** demain soir? Shall we go to the cinema tomorrow night?
lecture reading	La **lecture** est un passe-temps reposant. Reading is a relaxing pastime.
jeu vidéo video game	Je joue à des **jeux vidéo** en ligne. I play video games online.
console de jeux games console	Tu as quoi comme **console de jeux**? What kind of games console do you have?
télé(vision) television, TV	On regarde beaucoup la **télé(vision)** chez moi. We watch a lot of TV at home.
Internet internet	**Internet** est un outil formidable. The internet is a great tool.
dessin animé cartoon	Je regarde surtout des **dessins animés** à la télé. I watch mostly cartoons on TV.
film d'animation animation film	Les Japonais font de très bons **films d'animation**. The Japanese make very good animation films.
film d'horreur horror film	J'aime bien regarder des **films d'horreur**. I like watching horror films.

Le temps libre
Free time

documentaire documentary	Il y a des **documentaires** intéressants sur cette chaîne. There are interesting documentaries on this channel.
jeu télévisé game show	J'aimerais participer à un **jeu télévisé**. I would like to take part in a game show.
émission programme	C'est une **émission** sur l'Australie. It's a programme about Australia.
télé-réalité reality TV	Il y a une émission de **télé-réalité** ce soir. There is a reality TV programme on tonight.
magazine magazine	J'ai passé tout l'après-midi à lire des **magazines**. I spent all afternoon reading magazines.
roman novel	Je suis en train de lire un **roman** historique. I'm reading a historical novel.
jeu de société board game	Vous voulez jouer à un **jeu de société**? Do you want to play a board game?
puzzle jigsaw	On a mis une semaine à finir ce **puzzle**. It took us a week to finish this jigsaw.
(téléphone) portable mobile (phone)	Tous mes copains ont un **(téléphone) portable**. All my friends have a mobile (phone).
SMS, texto text (message)	Envoie-moi un **SMS/texto** quand tu seras prête. Send me a text (message) when you're ready.
vidéo video	Tu as vu cette **vidéo** sur YouTube? Have you seen this video on YouTube?
photo photography	Yohann fait de la **photo**, il est très doué. Yohann does photography – he's really good at it.

Les métiers
Jobs

travail work	Mon père va à Paris pour son **travail**. My father travels to Paris for his work.
profession occupation	Quelle est votre **profession**? What is your occupation?
bureau office	Il travaille dans un **bureau**. He works in an office.
acteur, actrice actor, actress	Carla rêve de devenir **actrice**. Carla dreams of becoming an actress.
footballeur, footballeuse footballer	Mon frère voudrait être **footballeur** professionnel. My brother would like to be a professional footballer.
chanteur, chanteuse singer	Les tournées sont fatigantes pour les **chanteurs**. Tours are tiring for singers.
musicien, musicienne musician	Mon grand frère a toujours voulu être **musicien**. My big brother has always wanted to be a musician.
développeur, développeuse (software) developer	Jack fait des études pour devenir **développeur**. Jack is studying to become a (software) developer.
graphiste graphic designer	Elle est **graphiste** dans la publicité. She's a graphic designer in advertising.
infirmier, infirmière nurse	Les **infirmières** travaillent parfois la nuit. Nurses sometimes work nights.
médecin, docteur doctor	**Médecin**, c'est un métier utile. Being a doctor is a useful job.

Les métiers
Jobs

vétérinaire vet	Je veux être **vétérinaire** comme ma mère. I want to be a vet like my mum.
avocat, avocate lawyer	Il faut faire de longues études pour devenir **avocat**. You have to study for a long time to become a lawyer.
professeur teacher	Mon cousin est **professeur** de physique. My cousin is a physics teacher.
styliste designer	Si tu aimes la mode, tu peux devenir **styliste**. If you like fashion, you can become a designer.
mannequin model	Quand on est **mannequin**, on voyage beaucoup. When you're a model you travel a lot.
journaliste journalist	Nicolas est **journaliste** à la télé. Nicolas is a journalist on TV.
architecte architect	Karim fait un stage chez un grand **architecte**. Karim is doing a work placement with a famous architect.
ingénieur engineer	Il y a peu de filles dans les écoles d'**ingénieurs**. There are few girls in engineering schools.
chef cuisinier, **chef cuisinière** chef	Les **chefs cuisiniers** font souvent des journées très longues. Chefs often work very long days.
pilote pilote	Le père d'Alice est **pilote** d'avion. Alice's dad is a pilot.
policier police officer	Je n'aimerais pas être **policier**. I wouldn't like to be a police officer.
pompier firefighter	Il y a des **pompiers** professionnels et des bénévoles. There are professional firefighters and volunteers.

Top tip: In French, when you say what your job is, you don't use the word for *a*, e.g. **elle est professeur** she's a teacher.

Au bord de la mer
At the seaside

plage beach	On se promène sur la **plage**. We are walking on the beach.
mer sea	Nager dans la **mer** peut être dangereux. Swimming in the sea can be dangerous.
vague wave	J'aime sauter dans les **vagues**. I like jumping in the waves.
sable sand	J'adore le **sable** chaud sous mes pieds. I love the hot sand beneath my feet.
serviette towel	La **serviette** est dans mon sac de plage. The towel is in my beach bag.
maillot de bain swimming costume/ trunks	Je porte un **maillot de bain** en dessous. I am wearing a swimming costume underneath.
crème solaire sun cream	Il faut mettre de la **crème solaire**. You must put sun cream on.
lunettes de soleil sunglasses	Je mets toujours mes **lunettes de soleil**. I always put my sunglasses on.
parasol sun umbrella	Maman dort sous un **parasol** de plage. Mum is sleeping under a sun umbrella.
chaise longue sunlounger	Je me détends sur une **chaise longue**. I am relaxing on a sunlounger.
château de sable sandcastle	Les enfants construisent des **châteaux de sable**. The children are building sandcastles.
seau bucket	Un homme ramasse des algues dans un **seau**. A man is collecting seaweed in a bucket.

Au bord de la mer
At the seaside

pelle spade	J'aime creuser des trous avec ma **pelle**. I like to dig holes with my spade.
pique-nique picnic	On fait un **pique-nique** sur la plage. We are having a picnic on the beach.
sports nautiques water sports	On a essayé plusieurs **sports nautiques** pendant les vacances. We tried several water sports during the holidays.
bateau boat	Je vois un petit **bateau** à l'horizon. I see a little boat on the horizon.
phare lighthouse	Il y a un **phare** sur la falaise. There is a lighthouse on the cliff.
falaise cliff	La plage est au pied d'une grande **falaise** blanche. The beach is at the foot of a big white cliff.
crabe crab	Un **crabe** se cache derrière un rocher. A crab is hiding behind a rock.
algues seaweed	La plage est couverte d'**algues**. The beach is covered in seaweed.
coquillage shell	Mon frère cherche des **coquillages**. My brother is looking for shells.
mouette seagull	Il y a beaucoup de **mouettes** au bord de la mer. There are lots of seagulls at the seaside.
méduse jellyfish	Papa a peur des **méduses**. Dad is frightened of jellyfish.
baleine whale	Mon frère a dit qu'il a vu une **baleine**. My brother said he saw a whale.

Les vacances et les voyages
Holidays and travel

mer seaside	On va en vacances à la **mer** cet été. We're going on holiday to the seaside this summer.
montagne mountains	J'ai passé une semaine à la **montagne**. I spent a week in the mountains.
ville city	J'aime visiter les grandes **villes**. I like to visit big cities.
campagne countryside	Les vacances à la **campagne** sont très reposantes. Holidays in the countryside are very relaxing.
touriste tourist	Le village est plein de **touristes**. The village is full of tourists.
monument monument	Le Colisée est un **monument** très impressionnant. The Colosseum is a very impressive monument.
musée museum/gallery	On a visité le **musée** des sciences/le **musée** des beaux-arts. We visited the science museum/the art gallery.
exposition exhibition	Vous avez aimé l'**exposition** sur les impressionnistes? Did you like the exhibition on the Impressionists?
château castle	Il y a un **château** en ruines sur la colline. There's a ruined castle on the hill.
parc à thème theme park	C'est le plus grand **parc à thème** du pays. It's the biggest theme park in the country.
visite guidée guided tour	La **visite guidée** dure une heure. The guided tour is an hour long.
lac lake	La maison est au bord d'un petit **lac**. The house is by a small lake.

Les vacances et les voyages
Holidays and travel

rivière river	On s'est baignés tous les jours dans la **rivière**. We swam in the river every day.
forêt forest	J'ai trouvé des champignons dans la **forêt**. I found some mushrooms in the forest.
camping campsite	Le **camping** est complet. The campsite is full.
faire du camping to camp	Je n'aime pas **faire du camping** quand il pleut. I don't like camping when it rains.
tente tent	Ils ont monté leur **tente** en dix minutes. They put up their tent in ten minutes.
caravane caravan	C'est une **caravane** pour quatre personnes. It's a caravan for four people.
hôtel hotel	L'**hôtel** est en face de la mairie. The hotel is opposite the town hall.
gîte self-catering cottage	On a réservé un **gîte** en Écosse. We have booked a self-catering cottage in Scotland.
village-vacances holiday village	On va chaque année dans le même **village-vacances**. We go to the same holiday village every year.
louer to rent/to hire	Vous avez **loué** un appartement/des vélos? Did you rent a flat/hire bikes?
promenade walk	J'aime faire des **promenades** au bord de la mer. I like to go for walks by the seaside.
randonnée hike	Elles sont parties en **randonnée** pour la journée. They've gone on a hike for the day.

Top tip: In French, the word **musée** can refer to both a *museum* and a *gallery*; **louer** can mean both *rent* (a flat) and *hire* (a car/bike).

voiture car	Ma **voiture** est garée devant la maison. My car is parked in front of the house.
aller/emmener en voiture to drive	Ma mère **va** au travail/m'**emmène** au collège **en voiture**. My mother drives to work/drives me to school.
vélo bicycle, bike	Benoît a un super **vélo** de course. Benoît has a great racing bike.
aller à vélo to cycle	On y **va à vélo**? Shall we cycle there?
autobus, bus bus	Le **bus** s'arrête juste devant le collège. The bus stops right in front of the school.
car coach	Les voyages scolaires se font toujours en **car**. School trips are always by coach.
train train	On est allés à Dijon en **train**. We went to Dijon by train.
avion plane	Tu as déjà pris l'**avion**? Have you ever been on a plane?
taxi taxi	Appelle un **taxi**, sinon on va être en retard. Call a taxi, otherwise we'll be late.
mobylette moped	Sonia est venue à **mobylette**. Sonia came on her moped.
moto motorbike	Il a une grosse **moto** noire. He has a big black motorbike.
à pied on foot	Tu préfères y aller en bus ou **à pied**? Would you rather go by bus or on foot?

Les moyens de transport
Means of transport

métro underground	Où est la station de **métro** la plus proche? Where is the nearest underground station?
tram(way) tram	Il y aura bientôt une nouvelle ligne de **tram(way)** à Nice. Soon there will be a new tram line in Nice.
bateau boat	Je suis malade en **bateau**. I get sick on boats.
ferry ferry	Il faut prendre le **ferry** pour aller dans l'île. You have to take the ferry to go to the island.
gare station	La **gare** est un peu plus loin sur la gauche. The station is a bit further on your left.
gare routière bus station	Le 114 part de la **gare routière** à sept heures trente. The 114 leaves from the bus station at seven thirty.
quai platform	De quel **quai** part le train pour Brest? Which platform does the train for Brest leave from?
salle d'attente waiting room	On est restés dans la **salle d'attente**. We stayed in the waiting room.
aéroport airport	Qui va nous emmener à l'**aéroport**? Who will take us to the airport?
terminal terminal	On part du **terminal** B. We're leaving from terminal B.
porte d'embarquement departure gate	Attendez à la **porte d'embarquement** D. Wait at departure gate D.
navette shuttle	Il y a une **navette** entre les terminaux. There's a shuttle between the terminals.

Vocabulaire

rue street	Prenez la deuxième **rue** à droite. Take the second street on the right.
trottoir pavement	Reste bien sur le **trottoir**. Make sure you stay on the pavement.
feu traffic lights	C'est à gauche au deuxième **feu**. It's on the left at the second set of traffic lights.
passage piéton pedestrian crossing	Traversez toujours au **passage piéton**. Always cross at the pedestrian crossing.
arrêt de bus bus stop	On se retrouve à trois heures à l'**arrêt de bus**. Let's meet at the bus stop at three o'clock.
zone piétonnière pedestrian area	La **zone piétonnière** commence ici. The pedestrian area starts here.
bâtiment building	Ce **bâtiment** date du dix-huitième siècle. This building dates back to the eighteenth century.
mairie town hall	Il faut demander à la **mairie**. You have to enquire at the town hall.
place square	Ils habitent près de la **place**. They live near the square.
jardin public park	Il y a un joli **jardin public** derrière l'école. There's a pretty park behind the school.
arbre tree	Il y a des **arbres** tout le long de la rue. There are trees all along the street.
école school	L'**école** est tout près d'ici. The school is very near here.

En ville
In town

restaurant restaurant	J'aime le **restaurant** chinois en ville. I like the chinese restaurant in town.
café café	C'est le **café** où mon frère retrouve ses copains. That's the café where my brother meets his friends.
pharmacie chemist's	Je dois passer à la **pharmacie** acheter des pansements. I have to pop into the chemist's to buy some plasters.
librairie bookshop	Tu crois qu'ils vendent des calendriers à la **librairie**? Do you think they sell calendars in the bookshop?
boulangerie bakery	On achète notre pain à la **boulangerie** près de chez nous. We get our bread from the bakery near our house.
pâtisserie cake shop	C'est la meilleure **pâtisserie** de la ville. It's the best cake shop in town.
boucherie butcher's	J'ai acheté du steak à la **boucherie**. I bought some steak from the butcher's.
marchand de fruits et légumes greengrocer	Il y a deux **marchands de fruits et légumes** au marché. There are two greengrocers at the market.
boutique de vêtements clothes shop	Les **boutiques de vêtements** ne sont pas terribles ici. The clothes shops aren't great here.
supermarché supermarket	On fait nos courses dans ce **supermarché**. We shop at this supermarket.
banque bank	À quelle heure ferme la **banque**? What time does the bank close?
poste post office	Tu peux m'acheter des timbres à la **poste**? Can you get me stamps from the post office?

Vocabulary

Les pays, les continents, les langues
Countries, continents, languages

la France France	J'habite en **France**. I live in France.
français, française French	Il a une copine **française**./J'apprends le **français**. He has a French girlfriend./I'm learning French.
l'Angleterre England	Tu connais bien **l'Angleterre**? Do you know England well?
anglais, anglaise English	J'adore les chips **anglaises**./J'apprends l'**anglais**. I love English crisps./I'm learning English.
la Grande-Bretagne Great Britain	**La Grande-Bretagne** comprend l'Angleterre, l'Écosse et le pays de Galles. Great Britain includes England, Scotland, and Wales.
britannique British	Les journaux **britanniques** en ont beaucoup parlé. British newspapers talked about it a lot.
l'Écosse Scotland	J'aimerais visiter **l'Écosse**. I'd like to visit Scotland.
écossais, écossaise Scottish	Aberdeen est une ville **écossaise**. Aberdeen is a Scottish city.
l'Irlande Ireland	J'ai passé un mois en **Irlande**. I spent a month in Ireland.
irlandais, irlandaise Irish	La campagne **irlandaise** est très jolie. The Irish countryside is very pretty.
le pays de Galles Wales	Il pleut beaucoup au **pays de Galles**. It rains a lot in Wales.
gallois, galloise Welsh	L'équipe de rugby **galloise** a battu la France. The Welsh rugby team beat France.

Les pays, les continents, les langues
Countries, continents, languages

l'Espagne Spain	On a décidé d'aller en vacances en **Espagne**. We decided to go on holiday to Spain.
espagnol, espagnole Spanish	Mon voisin est **espagnol**./J'apprends l'**espagnol**. My neighbour is Spanish./I'm learning Spanish.
l'Allemagne Germany	J'habite en Alsace, près de l'**Allemagne**. I live in Alsace, near Germany.
allemand, allemande German	J'ai une voiture **allemande**./J'apprends l'**allemand**. I have a German car./I'm learning German.
l'Italie Italy	On part pour l'**Italie** demain matin. We're leaving for Italy tomorrow morning.
italien, italienne Italian	J'adore les glaces **italiennes**./J'apprends l'**italien**. I love Italian ice cream./I'm learning Italian.
les États-Unis the United States	Notre prof d'anglais vient des **États-Unis**. Our English teacher comes from the United States.
la Chine China	**La Chine** est le pays le plus peuplé du monde. China is the most populated country in the world.
l'Europe Europe	**L'Europe** est beaucoup plus petite que l'Amérique. Europe is a lot smaller than America.
l'Amérique America	Tu es déjà allé en **Amérique**? Have you ever been to America?
l'Asie Asia	**L'Asie** est un continent qui m'attire beaucoup. Asia is a continent that appeals to me a lot.
l'Afrique Africa	Ils viennent d'**Afrique**. They come from Africa.

Top tip: In French, there are different ways of saying *in* or *to* according to the gender of the country: you say **en France** but **au pays de Galles**.

Spelling help

Prononciation et orthographe
Sounds and spellings

In French, some sounds can be spelled in several different ways. The most common of these are **/o/**, **/aw/**, **/e/**, and **/eh/**. The words in each cloud show the different groups of letters that can all have the same sound!

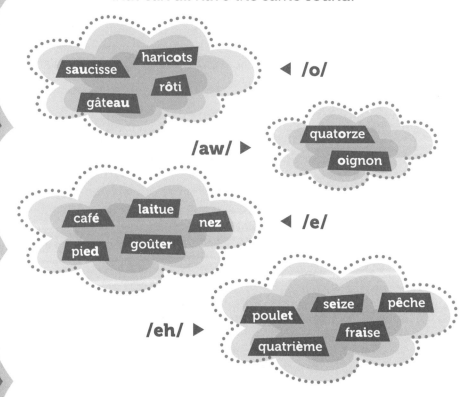

saucisse haricots rôti gâteau ◀ /o/

/aw/ ▶ quatorze oignon

café laitue nez pied goûter ◀ /e/

/eh/ ▶ poulet seize pêche fraise quatrième

To find the meanings of the words in the clouds,
look up pages 8, 16–20, and 24–25.

Word fun

Que suis-je?
What am I?

These anagrams are made from the names of animals that you have learned in this book (see pages 14–15). Solve the clues and unscramble the letters.

1. **PAÉLHTNÉ:** I am a huge animal with very large ears and a trunk. I live in Africa or Asia.

2. **NPALI:** I am a small animal with long ears and big front teeth. I can be wild or a pet.

3. **VLEHAC:** I am a large animal that people can ride. I can run very fast.

4. **EÈBZR:** I am a stripy cousin of the animal at number 3 above.

Que fais-je?
What's my job?

These anagrams are made from the names of jobs that you have learned in this book (see pages 44–45). Solve the clues and unscramble the letters.

1. **SOSPRUEFRE:** I teach children in secondary school or at university.

2. **NETIJRULAOS:** I write or talk about current affairs in the newspapers, on TV or on the radio.

3. **RIOPMEP:** I am a member of the emergency services that deal with fires.

4. **LIPETO:** I fly planes.

Answers:
What am I? – 1. **éléphant** elephant 2. **lapin** rabbit 3. **cheval** horse 4. **zèbre** zebra
What's my job? – 1. **professeur** teacher 2. **journaliste** journalist 3. **pompier** firefighter 4. **pilote** pilot

Now practise . . .

Faux amis
False friends

False friends are words that look the same as or very similar to English words that you know, but actually mean something else entirely. You have seen words like this in the previous pages.

large (Fr) = large ✗
large (Fr) = wide ✓

> *large* in English is **grand** in French

chips (Fr) = chips ✗
chips (Fr) = crisps ✓

> *chips* in English is **frites** in French

sensible (Fr) = sensible ✗
sensible (Fr) = sensitive ✓

> *sensible* in English is **raisonnable** in French

médecin (Fr) = medicine ✗
médecin (Fr) = doctor ✓

> *medicine* in English is **médicament** in French

librairie (Fr) = library ✗
librairie (Fr) = bookshop ✓

> *library* in English is **bibliothèque** in French

veste (Fr) = vest ✗
veste (Fr) = jacket ✓

> *vest* in English is **maillot de corps** in French

cave (Fr) = cave ✗
cave (Fr) = cellar ✓

> *cave* in English is **grotte** in French

Grammaire
Grammar

Les questions
Questions

que, qu'est-ce que what	**Que** fais-tu?/**Qu'est-ce que** tu fais? What are you doing?
qui who	**Qui** a mangé tout le chocolat? Who ate all the chocolate?
quand when	Le feu d'artifice commence **quand**? When do the fireworks begin?
pourquoi why	**Pourquoi** tes cheveux sont mouillés? Why is your hair wet?
comment how	**Comment** ça se dit en anglais? How do you say this in English?
où where	**Où** est mon stylo? Where is my pen?
quoi what	De **quoi** parle-t-elle? What is she talking about?
combien how much	**Combien** ça coûte? How much does it cost?
combien de how much/many	Tu as **combien** d'argent?/Tu as **combien de** frères? How much money do you have?/ How many brothers do you have?
quel, quelle, quels, quelles which	Tu veux **quel** dessert?/Tu aimes **quels** chanteurs? Which dessert do you want?/Which singers do you like?
lequel, laquelle, lesquels, lesquelles which one, which ones	**Laquelle** tu préfères?/**Lesquels** sont les meilleurs? Which one do you prefer?/Which ones are the best?

Les mots de liaison
Connecting words

et and	Pauline **et** Margot sont très copines. Pauline and Margot are great friends.
ou or	Tu veux des frites **ou** du riz? Do you want chips or rice?
mais but	Il est mignon **mais** pas très sympa. He's cute but not very friendly.
ni . . . ni not . . . or	Je n'aime **ni** le thé, **ni** le café. I don't like tea or coffee.
si if	Tu peux rester ici **si** tu veux. You can stay here if you want.
que that	Je sais **que** ce n'est pas vrai. I know (that) it isn't true.
parce que because	J'aime bien le prof d'anglais **parce qu'**il est rigolo. I like the English teacher because he's funny.
puisque since	On peut y aller **puisque** tout le monde est là. We can go since everyone is here.
pour que so that	Presse-toi **pour qu'**on parte à l'heure Hurry up so we can leave on time.
sinon otherwise, or	Dépêche-toi, **sinon** tu vas être en retard. Hurry up or you'll be late.
donc so	On a de l'argent, **donc** il n'y a pas de problème. We have money, so there's no problem.
même si even if	**Même si** tu cries, il ne t'entendra pas. Even if you shout, he won't hear you.

Top tip: Que in French is often not translated into English:
Je sais que ce n'est pas vrai. I know (that) it isn't true.

Comparer les gens et les choses
Comparing people and things

aussi . . . que as . . . as	Ce gratte-ciel est **aussi** grand **que** la tour Eiffel. This skyscraper is as tall as the Eiffel Tower.
autant que as much as	Je mange **autant que** mon frère. I eat as much as my brother.
moins . . . que less . . . than/ not as . . . as	Maman est **moins** inquiète **que** papa. Mum is less worried than/not as worried as Dad.
plus . . . que more . . . than/ . . . -er than	Kevin est **plus** bavard/rapide **que** Lucas. Kevin is more talkative/faster than Lucas.
meilleur, meilleure better	Il est **meilleur**/Elle est **meilleure** que moi en maths. He is better/She is better than me at maths.
mieux better	Tu te sens **mieux** aujourd'hui? Are you feeling better today?
pire worse	C'est encore **pire** quand il pleut! It's even worse when it rains!
le plus, la plus the most/the . . . -est	C'est **le plus** petit. C'est **la plus** intelligente. He's the smallest. She's the most intelligent.
le meilleur, la meilleure the best	Qui est **le meilleur** coureur du monde? Élodie est **la meilleure** en gym. Who is the best runner in the world? Élodie is the best at PE.
le pire, la pire the worst	C'est **le pire** film de tous les temps! Notre équipe a été **la pire** du tournoi. It's the worst film of all time! Our team was the worst in the tournament.

La quantité et l'intensité
Quantity and intensity

pas de no	Il n'y a **pas de** pain. There is no bread.
plus de no . . . left/no more . . .	Nous n'avons **plus d'**argent. We have no money left./We have no more money.
beaucoup a lot	Elle parle **beaucoup**. She talks a lot.
beaucoup de a lot of/much/many	Charles a **beaucoup de** copains. Il ne reste pas **beaucoup de** pain. Charles has a lot of/many friends. There isn't much bread left.
trop too much	J'ai **trop** mangé, j'ai mal au ventre. I've eaten too much, I have a stomach ache.
trop de too much/too many	On a **trop de** travail./J'ai fait **trop de** fautes. We have too much work./I made too many mistakes.
assez (de) enough	J'ai **assez** mangé./Tu as **assez de** couvertures? I've eaten enough./Do you have enough blankets?
peu not much	Je mange **peu**, une petite tranche suffira. I don't eat much, a small slice will be enough.
peu de not much/not many	Il reste **peu de** temps./**Peu de** gens le savent. There isn't much time left./Not many people know that.
un peu/un peu de a bit/a bit of	Je la connais **un peu**./Donnez-moi **un peu de** sucre. I know her a bit./Give me a bit of sugar.
très very	C'est **très** beau ici. It's very beautiful here.
vraiment really	Il faut **vraiment** que tu l'appelles. You really need to call him.

Top tip: In comparisons, you use **de** in French where you use *in* in English: **le meilleur coureur du monde** the best runner in the world.

Grammaire

avant before	Je fais des jeux vidéo **avant** le dîner. I play video games before dinner.
après after	On se retrouve dehors **après** le cours de géographie. Let's meet outside after the geography lesson.
pendant during	Charlotte a été malade **pendant** les vacances. Charlotte was ill during the holidays.
pendant que while	Reste ici **pendant que** je vais voir où il est. Stay here while I go and see where he is.
depuis since/for	On se connaît **depuis** 2012/**depuis** cinq ans. We've known each other since 2012/for five years.
jusqu'à, **jusqu'en** until	La soirée a duré **jusqu'à** 23 heures. Je serai au lycée **jusqu'en** 2018. The party lasted until 11 p.m. I'll be at secondary school until 2018.
quand when	On sortira **quand** il fera meilleur. We'll go out when the weather's better.
dans in	Ils déménagent **dans** trois jours. They're moving house in three days.
en in	Elle a mangé deux assiettes de pâtes **en** dix minutes! She ate two plates of pasta in ten minutes!
il y a ago	J'ai acheté cette tablette **il y a** un an. I bought this tablet a year ago.
dès que as soon as	Olivia m'a appelé **dès qu'**elle a eu mon texto. Olivia called me as soon as she got my text.

Le temps
Time

toujours always	Tu es **toujours** en retard! You're always late!
jamais never	Mon père ne me laisse **jamais** sortir le soir. My father never lets me go out at night.
souvent often	Il y a **souvent** du poulet à la cantine. We often get chicken for our school dinner.
rarement rarely	On se parle **rarement**. We rarely speak to each other.
maintenant now	On peut y aller **maintenant**, j'ai fini. We can go now, I've finished.
déjà already	Vous êtes **déjà** arrivées? Are you there already?
bientôt soon	Le cours est **bientôt** fini. The lesson will soon be over.
ensuite afterwards	On ira au cinéma et **ensuite** au restau. We'll go to the cinema and afterwards to a restaurant.
tard late	Je suis rentrée super **tard**. I got back really late.
tôt early	Tu te lèves **tôt** le matin? Do you get up early in the morning?
encore still	Quoi, tu es **encore** au lit! What, you're still in bed!

La position
Position

à, au, aux in/at/to	Je suis encore **à** l'école/On va **au** cinéma?/ Ils habitent **aux** États-Unis. I'm still at school./Shall we go to the cinema?/ They live in the United States.
dans in/into	Le beurre est **dans** le frigo./Monte **dans** la voiture. The butter is in the fridge./Get into the car.
sur on	Ton livre est **sur** la table. Your book is on the table.
sous under	Le chat se cache **sous** le lit. The cat is hiding under the bed.
devant in front of	Samira est assise **devant** moi en classe. Samira sits in front of me in class.
derrière behind	La gare est **derrière** la mairie. The train station is behind the town hall.
dessus on top	On a fait un gâteau avec du chocolat **dessus**. We made a cake with chocolate on top.
dessous underneath	Je porte un manteau et un pull **dessous**. I'm wearing a coat and a jumper underneath.
au-dessus de above	Regarde, il y a un papillon **au-dessus de** ta tête. Look, there's a butterfly above your head.
en face de opposite	L'arrêt de bus est **en face du** cinéma. The bus stop is opposite the cinema.
entre between	Assieds-toi **entre** Oscar et Émilie. Sit between Oscar and Emilie.

La position
Position

à côté de next to	La boulangerie est **à côté de** la pharmacie. The bakery is next to the chemist's.
contre against	Poussez l'armoire **contre** le mur. Push the wardrobe against the wall.
ici here	Où est Nathan? – **Ici!** Where's Nathan? – Here!
là there	Mets-toi **là.** Stand there.
là-bas over there	Elle est **là-bas**, tu la vois? She's over there, can you see her?
loin (de) far (from)	C'est trop **loin** pour rentrer à pied. Ils n'habitent pas **loin de** chez moi. It's too far to walk back. They don't live far from my house.
près (de) near	Le cinéma est tout **près (d'**ici). The cinema is very near (here).
vers towards	Ils ont couru **vers** les buts. They ran towards the goalposts.
par through	Passe **par** le village, c'est plus court. Go through the village, it's quicker.
jusqu'à/jusqu'au as far as	Il y a des embouteillages **jusqu'à** Strasbourg. Allez **jusqu'au** supermarché et tournez à gauche. There are traffic jams as far as Strasbourg. Go as far as the supermarket and turn left.

Les pronoms personnels
Personal pronouns

je, j' I	**Je** suis français./**J'**aime le chocolat. I'm French./I like chocolate.
tu you	**Tu** as des animaux? Do you have pets?
il he/it	**Il** a deux sœurs./J'aime ce pull, mais **il** est trop petit. He has two sisters./I like this jumper but it's too small.
elle she/it/her	**Elle** habite à Aix./J'aime cette jupe, **elle** est jolie. Samuel est amoureux d'**elle**. She lives in Aix./I like this skirt – it's pretty. Samuel is in love with her.
on we/one	**On** y va?/**On** ne sait jamais. Shall we go?/One never knows.
nous we/us/ourselves/ each other	**Nous** arriverons demain soir./Ils sont derrière **nous**. **Nous nous** sommes fait mal./**Nous nous** entraidons. We will arrive tomorrow night./They're behind us. We hurt ourselves./We help each other.
vous you/yourself/ yourselves/ each other	**Vous** voulez du fromage?/Je **vous** parlerai plus tard. **Vous vous** êtes fait mal?/**Vous vous** êtes vus? Do you want cheese?/I'll speak to you later. Did you hurt yourself (yourselves)?/Did you see each other?
ils they	**Ils** viennent d'Écosse. They come from Scotland.
elles they/them	**Elles** sont très sympas./J'y vais avec **elles**. They're very nice./I'm going with them.

Les pronoms personnels
Personal pronouns

me, m' me/myself	Tu **m'**énerves!/Je **me** suis regardé dans la glace. You're annoying me!/I looked at myself in the mirror.
te, t' you/yourself	Elle **te** regarde./Tu **t'**es fait mal? She's looking at you./Did you hurt yourself?
le, l' him/it	Je **le** trouve désagréable./La prof **l'**a puni. I find him (it) unpleasant./The teacher punished him.
la, l' her/it	Cette expo est géniale, va **la** voir. Abou **l'**attend à la sortie des cours. This exhibition is great, go and see it. Abou waits for her after school.
eux them	Et **eux**, ils sont partis?/Ce n'est pas pour **eux**. What about them, have they left?/It isn't for them.
lui him	C'est **lui** là-bas./On **lui** a parlé hier. That's him over there./We spoke to him yesterday.
leur to them	Je **leur** écrirai plus tard. I will write to them later.
se, s' himself/herself/ itself/themselves/ each other	Elle **s'**est présentée. Ils **se** sont acheté une console. Les chiens et les chats **se** détestent. She introduced herself. They bought themselves a console. Dogs and cats hate each other.

Top tip: Although the French word **on** looks like the English word *one*, in spoken French, it usually means *we*.

Les possessifs
Possessives

mon, ma, mes my	Tu connais **mon** père/**ma** mère/**mes** parents? Do you know my mum/my dad/my parents?
ton, ta, tes your	J'aime bien **ton** chien/**ta** tortue/**tes** poissons. I like your dog/your tortoise/your fish.
son, sa, ses his, her	Je lui ai emprunté **son** stylo. Je lui ai emprunté **sa** gomme. Je lui ai emprunté **ses** ciseaux. I borrowed his/her pen. I borrowed his/her rubber. I borrowed his/her scissors.
notre, nos our	Nous avons invité **notre** voisin/**nos** voisins. We invited our neighbour/our neighbours.
votre, vos your	Vous avez fait tomber **votre** magazine/**vos** lunettes. You dropped your magazine/your glasses.
leur, leurs their	Ils prennent **leur** dîner/**leurs** repas à la cuisine. They have their dinner/their meals in the kitchen.

Les possessifs
Possessives

le mien, la mienne, **les miens,** **les miennes** mine	Ce manteau est plus grand que **le mien.** Ces chaussures sont plus petites que **les miennes.** This coat is bigger than mine. These shoes are smaller than mine.
le tien, la tienne, **les tiens, les tiennes** yours	Tu es sûr que ce livre est **le tien?** Tu es sûr que ces clés sont **les tiennes?** Are you sure this book is yours? Are you sure these keys are yours?
le sien, la sienne, **les siens,** **les siennes** his, hers	Ce n'est pas ma place, c'est **la sienne.** Ce ne sont pas mes stylos, ce sont **les siens.** This isn't my seat, it's his. These aren't my pens, they're hers.
le nôtre, la nôtre, **les nôtres** ours	Cette idée est **la nôtre!** Ces idées sont **les nôtres!** This idea is ours! These ideas are ours!
le vôtre, la vôtre, **les vôtres** yours	Notre équipe est meilleure que **la vôtre.** Nos joueurs sont meilleurs que **les vôtres.** Our team is better than yours. Our players are better than yours.
le leur, la leur, **les leurs** theirs	J'aime le nôtre, mais pas **le leur.** J'aime les nôtres, mais pas **les leurs.** I like ours, but not theirs. I like ours, but not theirs.

Top tip: You use different words in French for possessive words like *my* e.g. **mon stylo** because **stylo** is masculine and **ma gomme** because **gomme** is feminine.

Les adjectifs: masculin et féminin
Adjectives: masculine and feminine

In French, most feminine adjectives are formed from the masculine following one of these rules.

masculine + -e	grand > grande **Benjamin est grand. > Amandine est grande.** Benjamin is tall. > Amandine is tall.
-er > -ère	premier > première **Il est toujours le premier à sortir. > Elle est toujours la première à sortir.** He's always the first one out. > She's always the first one out.
-e > -e	sympathique > sympathique **Henri est sympathique. > Adèle est sympathique.** Henri is friendly. > Adèle is friendly.
-el > -elle	actuel > actuelle **C'est son emploi du temps actuel/sa situation actuelle.** This is his current schedule/his current situation.
-en > -enne	parisien > parisienne **Il possède des théâtres parisiens/des entreprises parisiennes.** He owns Parisian theatres/Parisian companies.
-on > -onne	bon > bonne **Ce plat est très bon. > Cette soupe est très bonne.** This dish is very good. > This soup is very good.
-x > -se	délicieux > délicieuse **Ce plat est délicieux. > Cette soupe est délicieuse.** This dish is delicious. > This soup is delicious.
-eau > -elle	beau > belle **Ce bâtiment est très beau. > Cette maison est très belle.** This building is very beautiful. > This house is very beautiful.

Expressions avec 'avoir'
Expressions with 'avoir'

avoir faim to be hungry	**J'ai faim**, je veux manger tout de suite. I'm hungry, I want to eat straightaway.
avoir soif to be thirsty	Si tu **as soif**, je peux te donner de l'eau. If you're thirsty, I can give you some water.
avoir chaud to be hot	Ouvrez la fenêtre si vous **avez chaud**. Open the window if you're hot.
avoir froid to be cold	Brr, j'**ai froid**! Brrr, I'm cold!
avoir envie de to feel like	Elles n'**ont** pas **envie d**'aller à la piscine. They don't feel like going to the swimming pool.
avoir peur to be scared	Nous **avons eu peur** en entendant l'explosion. We were scared when we heard the explosion.
avoir besoin de to need	Appelle-moi si tu **as besoin de** quelque chose. Call me if you need anything.
avoir raison to be right	C'est vrai, tu **as raison**. That's true, you're right.
avoir tort to be wrong	Je reconnais que j'**ai eu tort**. I admit I was wrong.
avoir honte to be ashamed	J'**ai honte** de ne pas savoir nager. I'm ashamed because I can't swim.
avoir l'habitude de to be used to	Il **a l'habitude de** se lever tôt. He's used to getting up early.
avoir horreur de to hate	J'**ai horreur des** araignées. I hate spiders.
avoir de la chance to be lucky	Vous **avez de la chance**! You're lucky!

Top tip: None of the above expressions with **avoir** in French are translated with *have* in English.

Verbes réguliers
Regular verbs

1er groupe: chanter (verbs ending in -er)
1st group: to sing

Présent Present	Passé composé Past	Futur Future
je chante I sing	j'ai chanté I sang	je chanterai I will sing
tu chantes you sing	tu as chanté you sang	tu chanteras you will sing
il/elle/on chante he/she/it/one sings	il/elle/on a chanté he/she/it/one sang	il/elle/on chantera he/she/it/one will sing
nous chantons we sing	nous avons chanté we sang	nous chanterons we will sing
vous chantez you sing	vous avez chanté you sang	vous chanterez you will sing
ils/elles chantent they sing	ils/elles ont chanté they sang	ils/elles chanteront they will sing

Autres verbes réguliers du 1er groupe
Other regular verbs in the 1st group

adorer to love	**donner** to give	**habiter** to live	**porter** to carry, to wear
aimer to like	**écouter** to listen	**jouer** to play	
animer to run (a club, a camp)	**emmener** to take	**loger** to stay (in a hotel)	**préparer** to prepare
	étudier to study		**regarder** to look
arrêter to stop	**fermer** to close, to shut	**manger** to eat	**sauter** to jump
arriver to arrive	**frapper** to hit	**monter*** to go up	**travailler** to work
attraper to catch	**gagner** to win, to earn	**parler** to speak	**trouver** to find
détester to hate	**garder** to keep, to look	**passer** to go through	**visiter** to visit
discuter to talk	after	**plonger** to dive	**voyager** to travel

*This verb uses **être** and not **avoir** in the past tense and has different forms for masculine, feminine, and plural. See the note on page 75.

Verbes réguliers
Regular verbs

2e groupe: finir (verbs ending in -ir)
2nd group: to finish

Présent Present	Passé composé Past	Futur Future
je finis I finish	j'ai fini I finished	je finirai I will finish
tu finis you finish	tu as fini you finished	tu finiras you will finish
il/elle/on finit he/she/it/one finishes	il/elle/on a fini he/she/it/one finished	il/elle/on finira he/she/it/one will finish
nous finissons we finish	nous avons fini we finished	nous finirons we will finish
vous finissez you finish	vous avez fini you finished	vous finirez you will finish
ils/elles finissent they finish	ils/elles ont fini they finished	ils/elles finiront they will finish

Autres verbes réguliers du 2e groupe
Other regular verbs in the 2nd group

applaudir to clap	guérir to get better	réfléchir to think	rougir to blush
choisir to choose	maigrir to lose weight	remplir to fill up, to fill in	se salir to get dirty
grandir to grow	obéir to obey		vieillir to get old(er)
grossir to put on weight	ralentir to slow down	réussir to succeed, to pass (an exam)	vomir to vomit

*This verb uses **être** and not **avoir** in the past tense and has different forms for masculine, feminine, and plural, e.g.

je suis monté/montée	nous sommes montés/montées
tu es monté/montée	vous êtes monté/montée/montés/montées
il/on est monté/elle est montée	ils sont montés/elles sont montées

Verbes irréguliers
Irregular verbs

Présent Present		Passé composé Past		Futur Future	
aller* to go		être +			
vais	allons	allé(e)	allés(ées)	irai	irons
va	allez	allé(e)	allé(e)/ allés(ées)	iras	irez
va	vont	allé(e)	allés(ées)	ira	iront
apprendre to learn		avoir +			
apprends	apprenons	appris		apprendrai	apprendrons
apprends	apprenez			apprendras	apprendrez
apprend	apprennent			apprendra	apprendront
s'asseoir* to sit		être +			
m'assieds	nous asseyons	assis(e)	assis assises	m'assiérai	nous assiérons
t'assieds	vous asseyez	assis(e)	assis(e)/ assis(es)	t'assiéras	vous assiérez
s'assied	s'assoient	assis(e)	assis(es)	s'assiéra	s'assiéront
attendre to wait		avoir +			
attends	attendons	attendu		attendrai	attendrons
attends	attendez			attendras	attendrez
attend	attendent			attendra	attendront
avoir to have		avoir +			
ai	avons	eu		aurai	aurons
as	avez			auras	aurez
a	ont			aura	auront
boire to drink		avoir +			
bois	buvons	bu		boirai	boirons
bois	buvez			boiras	boirez
boit	boivont			boira	boiront
comprendre to understand		avoir +			
comprends	comprenons	compris		comprendrai	comprendrons
comprends	comprenez			comprendras	comprendrez
comprend	comprennent			comprendra	comprendront

Verbes irréguliers
Irregular verbs

Présent Present	Passé composé Past		Futur Future
connaître to know	avoir +		
connais connaissons connais connaissez connaît connaissent	connu		connaîtrai connaîtrons connaîtras connaîtrez connaîtra connaîtront
courir to run	avoir +		
cours courons cours courez court courent	couru		courrai courrons courras courrez courra courront
crier to shout	avoir +		
crie crions cries criez crie crient	crié		crierai crierons crieras crierez criera crieront
croire to believe	avoir +		
crois croyons crois croyez croit croient	cru		croirai croirons croiras croirez croira croiront
défaire to undo	avoir +		
défais défaisons défais défaites défait défont	défait		déferai déferons déferas déferez défera déferont
descendre* to go down	être +		
descends descendons descends descendez descend descendent	descendu(e) descendu(e) descendu(e)	descendus(es) descendu(e)/ descendus(es) descendu(s)(es)	descendrai descendrons descendras descendrez descendra descendront
devenir* to become	être +		
deviens devenons deviens devenez devient deviennent	devenu(e) devenu(e) devenu(e)	devenu(s)(es) devenu(e)/ devenus(es) devenu(s)(es)	deviendrai deviendrons deviendras deviendrez deviendra deviendront

*This verb uses **être** and not **avoir** in the past tense and has different forms for masculine, feminine, and plural. See the note on page 75.

Grammaire

Présent Present		Passé composé Past	Futur Future	
devoir must		avoir +		
dois	devons	dû	devrai	devrons
dois	devez		devras	devrez
doit	doivent		devra	devront
dire to say		avoir +		
dis	disons	dit	dirai	dirons
dis	dites		diras	direz
dit	disent		dira	diront
dormir to sleep		avoir +		
dors	dormons	dormi	dormirai	dormirons
dors	dormez		dormiras	dormirez
dort	dorment		dormira	dormiront
écrire to write		avoir +		
écris	écrivons	écrit	écrirai	écrirons
écris	écrivez		écriras	écrirez
écrit	écrivent		écrira	écriront
entendre to hear		avoir +		
entends	entendons	entendu	entendrai	entendrons
entends	entendez		entendras	entendrez
entend	entendent		entendra	entendront
espérer to hope		avoir +		
espère	espérons	espéré	espérerai	espérerons
espères	espérez		espéreras	espérerez
espère	espèrent		espérera	espéreront
être to be		avoir +		
suis	sommes	été	serai	serons
es	êtes		seras	serez
est	sont		sera	seront
faire to do/make		avoir +		
fais	faisons	fait	ferai	ferons
fais	faites		feras	ferez
fait	font		fera	feront

Verbes irréguliers
Irregular verbs

Présent Present		**Passé composé** Past		**Futur** Future	
falloir have to					
il faut		il a fallu		il faudra	
se lever* to get up		être +			
me lève	nous levons	levé(e)	levés(ées)	me lèverai	nous lèverons
te lèves	vous levez	levé(e)	levé(e)/levés(ées)	te lèveras	vous lèverez
se lève	se lèvent	levé(e)	levés(ées)	se lèvera	se lèveront
lire to read		avoir +			
lis	lisons	lu		lirai	lirons
lis	lisez			liras	lirez
lit	lisent			lira	liront
mettre to put		avoir +			
mets	mettons	mis		mettrai	mettrons
mets	mettez			mettras	mettrez
met	mettent			mettra	mettront
mourir* to die		être +			
meurs	mourons	mort(e)	morts(es)	mourrai	mourrons
meurs	mourez	mort(e)	mort(e)/morts(es)	mourras	mourrez
meurt	meurent	mort(e)	morts(es)	mourra	mourront
naître* to be born		être +			
nais	naissons	né(e)	nés(ées)	naîtrai	naîtrons
nais	naissez	né(e)	né(e)/nés(ées)	naîtras	naîtrez
naît	naissent	né(e)	nés(ées)	naîtra	naîtront
ouvrir to open		avoir +			
ouvre	ouvrons	ouvert		ouvrirai	ouvrirons
ouvres	ouvrez			ouvriras	ouvrirez
ouvre	ouvrent			ouvrira	ouvriront
partir* to leave		être +			
pars	partons	parti(e)	partis(es)	partirai	partirons
pars	partez	parti(e)	parti(e)/partis(es)	partiras	partirez
part	partent	parti(e)	partis(es)	partira	partiront

*This verb uses **être** and not **avoir** in the past tense and has different forms for masculine, feminine, and plural. See the note on page 75.

79

Présent Present		Passé composé Past	Futur Future	
payer to pay		avoir +		
paie *or* paye	payons	payé	paierai *or* payerai	paierons *or* payerons
paies *or* payes	payez		paieras *or* payeras	paierez *or* payerez
paie *or* paye	paient *or* payent		paiera *or* payera	paieront *or* payeront
perdre to lose		avoir +		
perds	perdons	perdu	perdrai	perdrons
perds	perdez		perdras	perdrez
perd	perdent		perdra	perdront
pleuvoir to rain				
il pleut		il a plu	il pleuvra	
pouvoir be able to		avoir +		
peux	pouvons	pu	pourrai	pourrons
peux	pouvez		pourras	pourrez
peut	peuvent		pourra	pourront
prendre to take		avoir +		
prends	prenons	pris	prendrai	prendrons
prends	prenez		prendras	prendrez
prend	prennent		prendra	prendront
rendre to give back		avoir +		
rends	rendons	rendu	rendrai	rendrons
rends	rendez		rendras	rendrez
rend	rendent		rendra	rendront
répondre to answer		avoir +		
réponds	répondons	répondu	répondrai	répondrons
réponds	répondez		répondras	répondrez
répond	répondent		répondra	répondront

Verbes irréguliers
Irregular verbs

Présent Present		Passé composé Past		Futur Future	
revenir* to come back		être +			
reviens	revenons	revenu(e)	revenus(es)	reviendrai	reviendrons
reviens	revenez	revenu(e)	revenu(e)/ revenus(es)	reviendras	reviendrez
revient	reviennent	revenu(e)	revenus(es)	reviendra	reviendront
rire to laugh		avoir +			
ris	rions	ri		rirai	rirons
ris	riez			riras	rirez
rit	rient			rira	riront
savoir to know		avoir +			
sais	savons	su		saurai	saurons
sais	savez			sauras	saurez
sait	savent			saura	sauront
sortir* to go out		être +			
sors	sortons	sorti(e)	sortis(es)	sortirai	sortirons
sors	sortez	sorti(e)	sorti(e)/sortis(es)	sortiras	sortirez
sort	sortent	sorti(e)	sortis(es)	sortira	sortiront
suffire to be enough					
ça suffit		ça a suffi		ça suffira	
suivre to follow		avoir +			
suis	suivons	suivi		suivrai	suivrons
suis	suivez			suivras	suivrez
suit	suivent			suivra	suivront
tenir to hold		avoir +			
tiens	tenons	tenu		tiendrai	tiendrons
tiens	tenez			tiendras	tiendrez
tient	tiennent			tiendra	tiendront

*This verb uses **être** and not **avoir** in the past tense and has different forms for masculine, feminine, and plural. See the note on page 75.

Présent Present		Passé composé Past		Futur Future	
valoir to be worth		avoir +			
vaux	valons	valu		vaudrai	vaudrons
vaux	valez			vaudras	vaudrez
vaut	valent			vaudra	vaudront
vendre to sell		avoir +			
vends	vendons	vendu		vendrai	vendrons
vends	vendez			vendras	vendrez
vend	vendent			vendra	vendront
venir* to come		être +			
viens	venons	venu(e)	venus(es)	viendrai	viendrons
viens	venez	venu(e)	venu(e)/ venus(es)	viendras	viendrez
vient	viennent	venu(e)	venus(es)	viendra	viendront
vivre to live		avoir +			
vis	vivons	vécu		vivrai	vivrons
vis	vivez			vivras	vivrez
vit	vivent			vivra	vivront
voir to see		avoir +			
vois	voyons	vu		verrai	verrons
vois	voyez			verras	verrez
voit	voient			verra	verront
vouloir to want		avoir +			
veux	voulons	voulu		voudrai	voudrons
veux	voulez			voudras	voudrez
veut	veulent			voudra	voudront

*This verb uses **être** and not **avoir** in the past tense and has different forms for masculine, feminine, and plural. See the note on page 75.

Word fun

La position
Position

Think of the position words you have learned in this book. You can build new sentences by using different position words in the sentences you have read. Look at the sentences below and try to choose the right word from each cloud to make a new sentence. You can look at pages 66–67 to help you.

1. Ton livre est **sur** la table.
Your book is on the table.

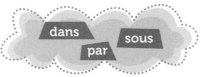

2. L'arrêt de bus est **en face du** cinéma.
The bus stop is opposite the cinema.

3. Il y a des embouteillages **jusqu'à** Strasbourg.
There are traffic jams as far as Strasbourg.

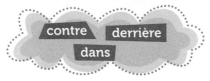

Now practise . . .

Les verbes réfléchis
Reflexive verbs

You normally use reflexive verbs to talk about an action you do to yourself. To do this, you use a pronoun like **me** or **se** with the verb in question. For example, Je **me** suis regardé dans la glace = I looked at **myself** in the mirror. These pronouns are often not translated in English, or sometimes the verb can be translated by *get* and an adjective.

Have a look at the examples below and try to match the verbs in the cloud to the sentences:

1. Je **me** lave = I wash (myself) *or* I have a wash.
2. Réveille-**toi**! = Wake (yourself) up!
3. Ne **te** moque pas de moi! = Don't (you) make fun of me!
4. Habille-**toi** vite. = Get (yourself) dressed quickly.
5. On **s'**est perdus. = We got (ourselves) lost.
6. Ne **vous** énervez pas. = Don't get (yourselves) annoyed.

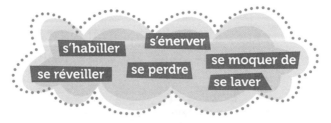

s'habiller
s'énerver
se réveiller
se perdre
se moquer de
se laver

Conversation
Conversation

Comment ça va?
How are you?

Q **(Comment) ça va?**
How are you?

A **Très bien, merci./Pas mal, et toi?**
Very well, thank you./Not bad, what about you?

Q **Comment tu te sens?**
How are you feeling?

A **Ça va un peu mieux.**
Je ne me sens pas très bien, j'ai toujours mal à la tête.
I'm a bit better.
I don't feel very well – I've still got a headache.

Q **Ça va mieux ton rhume?**
Is your cold better?

A **Oui, beaucoup mieux./Non, j'ai toujours le nez bouché.**
Yes, much better./No, I still have a stuffy nose.

Q **La soirée s'est bien passée?**
Did the party go well?

A **Oui, très bien, on s'est beaucoup amusés.**
Bof . . . Je me suis un peu ennuyé./Non, c'était nul!
Yes, very well, we had a great time.
Not really. . . I was a bit bored./No, it was rubbish!

Q **Tu es content de ton nouveau vélo?**
Are you happy with your new bike?

A **Oui, il est super./Non, j'ai un problème avec les freins.**
Yes, it's great./No, I have a problem with the brakes.

Rencontrer quelqu'un
Meeting someone

Q **Comment tu t'appelles?**
What's your name?

A **Je m'appelle Lucas/Clémentine.**
My name is Lucas/Clémentine.

Q **Tu as quel âge?**
How old are you?

A **J'ai onze ans/treize ans et demi.**
I'm eleven/thirteen and a half.

Q **Tu habites où?**
Where do you live?

A **J'habite à Paris/en France/à la campagne.**
I live in Paris/in France/in the country.

Q **Tu habites dans une maison?**
Do you live in a house?

A **Oui, une maison dans un village.**
Non, j'habite dans un appartement.
Yes, a house in a village/No, I live in a flat.

Q **Tu as un animal?**
Do you have a pet?

A **Oui, j'ai un cochon d'Inde/un chat/une tortue.**
Non, mes parents n'en veulent pas.
Yes, I have a guinea pig/a cat/a tortoise.
No, my parents don't want one.

La famille
Family

Q **Tu as des frères et sœurs?**
Do you have any brothers and sisters?

A **Oui, j'ai une grande sœur/un petit frère.**
Non, je suis fils unique.
Yes, I have an older sister./a younger brother.
No, I'm an only child.

Q **Quel métier font tes parents?**
Ta mère fait quoi comme métier?
What do your parents do?
What does your mum do?

A **Mon père est ingénieur et ma mère est professeur de maths.**
Elle ne travaille pas.
My dad's an engineer and my mum's a maths teacher.
She doesn't work.

Q **Tu vois souvent tes grands-parents?**
Do you often see your grandparents?

A **Oui, parce qu'ils habitent tout près.**
Non, je les vois rarement.
Yes, because they live very close by.
No, I rarely see them.

Q **Comment est ton frère/ta sœur?**
What's your brother/sister like?

A **Il est maigre et plus grand que moi.**
Elle est timide mais assez sympa.
He's skinny and taller than me.
She's shy but quite nice.

Les goûts et les opinions
Likes, dislikes, and opinions

Q **Quel est ton jeu vidéo préféré?**
What's your favourite video game?

A **C'est Minecraft; j'y joue tout le temps.**
Portal, parce que j'aime bien résoudre des énigmes.
It's Minecraft; I play it all the time.
Portal, because I like solving puzzles.

Q **Tu préfères les jupes ou les pantalons?**
Do you prefer skirts or trousers?

A **Ça dépend s'il fait chaud ou froid.**
Les pantalons, parce que c'est plus pratique.
It depends on whether the weather's hot or cold.
Trousers, because they're more practical.

Q **Qu'est-ce que tu penses du prof de français?**
What do you think of the French teacher?

A **Je l'aime bien, il est sympa./Je le trouve ennuyeux.**
I quite like him, he's nice./I find him boring.

Q **À ton avis, quel top je prends, le bleu ou le noir?**
What do you think? Which top should I take, blue or black?

A **Je ne sais pas trop./Je ne suis pas sûre.**
Je pense que le bleu te va mieux.
I don't really know./I'm not sure.
I think the blue one suits you better.

Q **Tu crois que Nadège aime bien Lionel?**
Do you think Nadège likes Lionel?

A **D'après moi, ils sont juste copains./Oui, il me semble.**
In my opinion, they're just friends./Yes, I think so.

Top tip: Maman and **papa** are only used by young children or to address your parents directly; to say *my mum/dad*, you say **ma mère/mon père.**

L'heure
Time

Q **Il est quelle heure?**
What time is it?

A **Il est trois heures./Il est une heure moins le quart.**
It's three o'clock./It's quarter to one.

Q **À quelle heure vous êtes rentrés?**
What time did you get back?

A **On est rentrés à dix-huit heures/vers deux heures et demie.**
We got back at six p.m./around half past two.

Q **Vous partez quand en voyage scolaire?**
When are you going on your school trip?

A **On part dans deux semaines/en juin/le mois prochain.**
We're leaving in two weeks/in June/next month.

Q **Tu habites ici depuis longtemps?**
Have you lived here long?

A **Non, depuis l'année dernière./Oui, j'ai toujours habité ici.**
No, since last year./Yes, I've always lived here.

Q **Tu vas souvent au bowling?**
Do you often go bowling?

A **Non, j'y vais rarement./Oui, à peu près une fois par mois.**
No, I rarely go./Yes, about once a month.

Q **Vous allez rester jusqu'à quand?**
Until when are you staying?

A **On va rester jusqu'à mardi/jusqu'à la semaine prochaine.**
We're going to stay until Tuesday/until next week.

Les loisirs
Free time

Q **Qu'est-ce que tu fais le week-end/pendant ton temps libre?**
What do you do at weekends/in your free time?

A **Je vais en ville avec mes copines.**
J'aime bien aller au cinéma./Je fais du dessin.
I go into town with my friends.
I like going to the cinema./I draw.

Q **Qu'est-ce que tu as prévu pour les vacances?**
What have you got planned for the holidays?

A **Je vais aller à la maison des jeunes.**
Je vais retrouver mes copains au centre commercial.
I'm going to go to the youth club.
I'm going to meet my friends at the shopping centre.

Q **Tu fais quoi quand tu n'as pas de devoirs?**
What do you do when you don't have any homework?

A **Je discute avec mes copines sur Whatsapp®.**
J'écoute de la musique sur mon portable.
I chat with my friends on Whatsapp®.
I listen to music on my mobile.

Q **Tu fais des activités après l'école?**
Do you do any activities after school?

A **Oui, je prends des cours de guitare.**
Non, je suis trop fatigué.
Yes, I take guitar lessons./No, I'm too tired.

Top tip: You can use different expressions to tell the time: **une heure moins le quart** quarter to one is also **douze heures quarante-cinq** twelve forty-five.

La nourriture
Food

Q **Quel est ton plat préféré?**
What is your favourite dish?

A **Les pâtes/Les saucisses/Les œufs/Le poulet.**
Pasta/Sausages/Eggs/Chicken.

Q **Qu'est-ce que tu bois au petit déjeuner?**
What do you drink for breakfast?

A **Je bois du thé/du café/du chocolat chaud/du jus de fruit.**
I drink tea/coffee/hot chocolate/fruit juice.

Q **Tu veux un sandwich à quoi?**
What do you want in your sandwich?

A **Au fromage/Au jambon-beurre.**
Cheese/Ham with butter.

Q **Qu'est-ce que vous prendrez comme plat principal?**
What would you like as a main course?

A **Je prendrai les spaghettis aux fruits de mer.**
I'll have the seafood spaghetti.

Q **Qu'est-ce que vous prendrez comme dessert?**
What would you like for dessert?

A **Je prendrai le gâteau au chocolat, s'il vous plaît.**
I'll have the chocolate cake, please.

Les vacances
Holidays

Q Tu es allé(e) où en vacances?
Where did you go on holiday?

A Je suis allé(e) à Paris/à la plage/à la montagne.
I went to Paris/to the seaside/to the mountains.

Q Tu as passé de bonnes vacances?
Did you have a good holiday?

A Oui, c'était super bien./C'était moyen.
Non, je me suis ennuyé(e).
Yes, it was great./It was all right.
No, I was bored.

Q Vous avez eu beau temps pendant les vacances?
Did you have good weather during the holidays?

A Oui, il a fait très beau./Non, il a plu tout le temps.
Yes, the weather was beautiful./No, it rained all the time.

Q Qu'est-ce que tu vas faire pendant les grandes vacances?
What are you going to do in the summer holidays?

A Je vais trouver un travail/aller voir mes grands-parents/
faire un stage de surf.
I'm going to find a job/visit my grandparents/
take surfing lessons.

Q Vous avez logé où quand vous êtes allés en Bretagne?
Where did you stay when you went to Brittany?

A On a logé à l'hôtel/a loué un gîte/a fait du camping.
We stayed in a hotel/rented a self-catering cottage/camped.

Top tip: In some French regions and French-speaking countries, the morning meal is called **déjeuner**, the midday meal **dîner**, and the evening meal **souper**.

Now practise...

Parler d'un livre ou d'un film
Talking about a book or a film

You can practise more conversations with your friends or in class using the words you have learned in this book. For example, talk about a book you've read or a film you've seen.

▶ Here are some words to get you started.

adorer

aimer

détester

super

bien

intéressant

nul

méchant

gentil

désagréable

rigolo

qualité

défaut

sympa

◀ To describe the characters, you can use the following words.

ville

campagne

mer

montagne

forêt

lac

rivière

▶ To describe the setting, you can use the following words.

Now practise. . .

Parler d'une fête d'anniversaire
Talking about a birthday party

You can practise more conversations with your friends or in class using the words you have learned in this book. For example, talk about what you did at a birthday party.

▶ Here are some words to get you started.

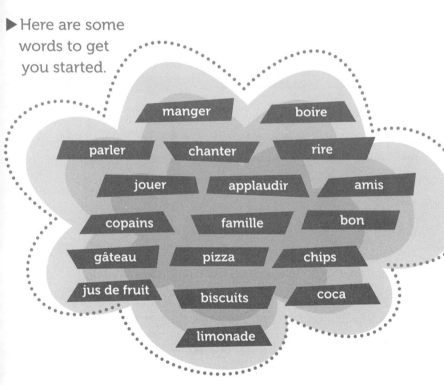

manger boire

parler chanter rire

jouer applaudir amis

copains famille bon

gâteau pizza chips

jus de fruit biscuits coca

limonade

For the words in the clouds and more, look at pages 16–18, 26–31, and 48–49. More adjectives are given on page 72 and verbs on pages 74–82.

Also available:

Age 5+

Age 5+

Age 7+

Age 10+

Age 10+

Age 11+

For core curriculum teaching materials:

Age 11+

Age 11+